Husbands

LISTEN

To Your Wives

S.B. Redd

Xpress Yourself
PUBLISHING

Xpress Yourself Publishing, LLC
P. O. Box 1615
Upper Marlboro, Maryland 20773

HUSBANDS, LISTEN TO YOUR WIVES

All Xpress Yourself Publishing titles are available at special quantity discounts for bulk purchases for sales, promotions, premiums, fund-raising, educational or institutional use. For more information, contact our sales department at (301) 390-3645 or e-mail us at info@xpressyourselfpublishing.com.

To receive a free weekly e-mail newsletter about our authors and titles we publish, register directly at our Web site at www.XpressYourselfPublishing.com for more great titles.

ISBN-13: 978-0-9845273-2-8

Library of Congress Control Number: 2010928076

Printed in the United States of America

First edition.

Cover and Interior Designed by The Writer's Assistant
For more information, visit www.thewritersassistant.com.

TABLE OF CONTENTS

Author's Note

I'm sure there are people who would find it utterly surprising that I would be inspired to write a series of books on relationships. Perhaps there is some truth that the people you least expect are the ones who come forth with such passion. It's like the person seen as a drunken degenerate who gets his life together and transforms himself into an outstanding citizen.

In my case, I had been in one failed marriage and nearly sunk a second one. My first marriage ended in divorce; because firstly, I had no business in that marriage. Admittedly, it was one of the worst decisions that I ever made in my adult life to have entered into some form of relationship, and then exacerbate it even more by asking her to marry me. So we live and we learn. That's been a lesson that I've been paying for a long, long time.

For many years, I resisted and rebelled against many good, sound suggestions offered by my current wife, whom I've known for about one-third of my life. My wife is not anyone's pushover. She holds her ground as firm as anyone I've ever known. But my wife is also the only person here on earth—other than our daughter—who can attest to the fact that I've made a sincere, heart-felt effort to turn things around for the good.

My wife will tell anybody who'd listen to her that she met me as a writer and she married me as a writer. She knows my ability to communicate in both the written and verbal forms are what I do best. Years ago while we maintained a network of people over the Internet, I once wrote an essay titled *Husbands, Listen to Your Wives.* Unfortunately, I don't have the original text of that essay. But some things remain etched in my heart. Hence, all the aforementioned have produced the confluence of experience, thoughts, and ideas that has enabled me to write this book.

I'm known as The Maverick to many. There's a reason for that. I've always tried blazing my own paths via my own way of thinking, and if I don't agree with you it may not be a good day for you. As an author of fiction, I've pushed my readers' literary envelope with an in-your-face brand of writing that one reviewer described me as an "author like none."

I think people like me are called rebels because we also have innate irreverent tendencies, but I'll stop just short of making such an admission because I've also learned after all these years that there is never anything new under the sun. You just try to do things better than the other person. I hope that you'll find that this book is not just any relationship book, because I'm aware that there are many out there.

SBR
www.maverick-books.com
www.maverick-media.ning.com
www.blogtalkradio.com/maverick-media

A Lesson Revisited

Although this book is written to enhance marriage relationships, I strongly believe it can help prepare men and women for that lasting, committed relationship that is called marriage; or if for anything else, help individuals to thrive in a relationship because they've been equipped with another important nugget.

I was in my late thirties at the time I wrote that essay titled *Husbands, Listen to Your Wives.* I was a little more than three years into my current marriage, but my wife and I had already gone through our share of ups and downs. We were in what I would describe as a period of repair, and I was in a state of moral remission. I learned years later that my wife harbored many underlying issues against me. There were also many things that I was not willing to admit to her as wrong nor make an honest effort at repairing. So what I managed to produce was hollow.

Over the years, we learn of other people's marital situations. The scenarios that I'm about to present to you is actually a mixture of many, but I think within them you may be able to identify with some or all of the issues described.

It seems to me that a marriage can run afoul at any point. Consider within a week of their wedding a couple is mired in a series of arguments that never should have arisen. Let's say that a wife discovers that her husband has maintained unacceptable contact with various women without regard to any sense of respect for his wife's feelings or their marriage. It is probable the wife felt that her husband's contact with the women should have ceased before he said, "I do" to her. But he vehemently argues that those women were his friends, and his wife has no right whatsoever to tell him whom he should maintain friendships or lines of communication with.

Disappointed by his reaction, the wife points out to her husband that he's still maintaining a single man's mindset and corresponding desire to engage in facets of a single man's lifestyle, although he'd gone through the process of having become a married man. He's incensed even more and he argues, resists harder, and yells at her louder than he did before. He advises her again, in no uncertain terms, to mind her business, and his contact with these women has nothing to do with her. Just leave him alone, he huffs.

The irony to his request about being left alone is that his actions are likely to produce the very result that he desires. For him, that may occur when he's feeling a sudden surge of hormones that he wants to act upon with his wife's cooperation. Because he refused to respect his wife's wishes and desires – guess what – she's not a willing participant and he's left with dealing with those unfulfilled desires of his—alone—and on many subsequent occasions.

It would be unfair to imply that this husband was a victim. But let's presume that he eventually admits that he failed at effectively handling what he thought were moments of rejection. Thus, he elected to seek more than just communication with some of those women that he maintained contact. The problems as described in this scenario persist in many relationships. And if you think that situation is bad, let's say that it gets worse. Now imagine that couple arguing over the fact that the husband has shown no willingness to wear his wedding ring. He explains to her that he often feels discomfort wearing it, which may or may not be true. However, his wife reminds him that it sends a message to others that he's showing no respect for his marriage.

The arguments escalate and they occur at intervals that are more frequent. Once again, and in no uncertain terms, he tells his wife to buzz off, leave him alone, and mind her business. Eventually, he yields to temptation and brings another woman into the picture, and it goes beyond just casual conversation. They become sexually involved. The inappropriate contact has developed into a full-blown adulterous relationship. That marriage is on unstable ground.

Here's another scenario that I could only nod my head and lament for the husband: He'd been on his job for nearly seven years. He always felt he was just a phone call away from a big promotion. Then the universe would be properly aligned and life would be great—at least in his opinion.

The desire to receive that phone call concerning his upward mobility was what kept him always on edge and motivated to perform at his best. The husband worked himself senseless, and there were many times in which he was not the best person to be around. A promotion would enable him to get a new start, including a divorce, and move on.

During those turbulent times, it was described to me that the wife would say, "Do you think you're going to get where you want treating me the way you're treating me?" To which the husband derided his wife.

"You're just jealous," he'd sneer back at her. "You just don't want to see me succeed at anything. I'll prove you wrong and anyone else who thinks that way about me!"

"I'm not against you," she would say. "You can't expect for things to go your way if you're treating me just any way."

Needless to say those were fighting—and sometimes cursing—words.

Now here's a bit of irony to all this. As much as the husband later confided in me that he wanted out of his marriage, a part of him felt he needed to stay in it. He felt he had a responsibility to reverse generations of broken relationships and marriages that he was aware of in his family:

- His parents separated and were divorced by the time he was ten. He learned that his mother had actually married and divorced twice. Within a matter of weeks after his parents were separated his mother had allowed another man to sleep with her—in her home—and his sister and him—ages five and seven, respectively—were stunned to see some stranger walking into their living room to greet them. He said that same man fathered their youngest sister two years later.

- His father had been married five times, divorced four. He was never known for his fidelity with his spouses. He was also known for a female acquaintance or two between his divorces.

- His maternal grandparents were a picture of stability. I always heard him say good things about them. They were married for more than thirty years until his grandfather's death.

- His other set of grandparents were never legally divorced, but as the story goes his grandfather left his grandmother and three young children after World War II. It was not the best of times for the grandmother who was quite young herself.

I told the guy that I could relate to him on many levels. Inwardly, I thought about how I had promised myself that I would treat a woman better than the way I saw my mother being treated by men. The best male example that I probably had during my childhood was my scoutmaster. Yes, I was a Boy Scout, and I earned the rank of Eagle Scout. My scoutmaster said at my Eagle Scout ceremony, "Every scoutmaster would like to say he had an Eagle Scout. Today I can say that." Years later, I had an opportunity to visit and thank him for the time he sacrificed for a bunch of unruly characters that comprised my scout troop.

The rest of the male examples that I had was guys whom I knew at the bowling alleys and race track that caroused and chased women. I thought they were the coolest men on earth because they were able to string women along and boast of their sexual conquests. That was the kind of guy that I wanted to become.

Therefore, by the time I became actively involved with women my idea of a successful relationship was the ability to possess the necessary skill to maintain sexual relations with a woman on my terms. It also involved no consideration for a woman's feelings or any significant measure of respect. Anything that went against my personal agenda was grounds for moving on—which I did quite regularly.

There were moments when arguments between my wife and I reached their frenetic apex that she would tell me to leave for the last time; however, there was something within that implored me not to do it. I knew deep within that marriage was the second most important confession that a person will ever make after a confession of faith (i.e., salvation).

I did share with him that on many occasions I often felt my loneliest during or after I had put myself in situations that were contrary to my marriage. It's sort of like sin and the separation it causes between us and God. I told him that I was never a party animal or carouser at the bars. But in my own warped ways, looking back, I often resorted to inappropriate behavior as my way of dealing with my low moments. I knew better, yet I ventured down paths where I knew I had no business.

As we talked further, I could sense the exasperation in his voice about his marriage. He confided in me that he'd given himself a month, and if things didn't get any better he was gone. The more we talked the more it seemed to me that I had a unique opportunity to essentially take a step back and see just how far I had once gone in my marriage. He had resigned himself into thinking that being twice divorced wasn't a bad thing. After all, some people don't get it right until their third marriage—or divorce—and by then they're willing to do whatever it takes to make sure that marriage doesn't fail.

At that moment, I told him that I once reached a similar point of despair as well. It may have been a force beyond my own will. I don't know. It might have even been divine revelation. But it dawned upon me that many of the people whom I had previously esteemed as friends had never meant me any good. Many of the people who had smiled in my face had only wished bad things for me both professionally and personally. And maybe, just maybe, the woman whom I had resisted and fought might be the only person who meant me any good.

I described to him how the change in me was immediate, and it did steer my marriage in a more positive direction. He thanked me for the information. But we've not spoken since then. So I don't have any idea whether he and his wife actually divorced, or turned things around in their marriage.

While reading the story about Abraham and Sarah I discovered that there was something divinely important about a husband listening to his wife. Most of us are familiar with the part that Abraham was the man whom God told to leave his country and move to a place that he did not know. God promised that he would make Abraham the father of many nations. Abraham reminded God that he did not have a child who would be the heir to the wealth that he'd amassed. God said that surely Abraham, who was seventy-five at the time, would produce a child despite the fact that he and Sarah were childless.

It is noted that Sarah and Abraham became impatient after more than twelve years, and at her suggestion, he had relations with one of his servants, Hagar, which resulted in the birth of Ishmael. Several years later Sarah felt disrespected by Hagar and she urged Abraham to evict Hagar. Abraham resisted, but God told him to listen to Sarah (Genesis 21:12).

"'Do not let it be displeasing in your sight because of the lad or because of your bondwoman. Whatever Sarah has said to you, listen to her voice; for in Isaac your seed shall be called.'"

It was from that passage that I was inspired to write that initial essay. I wrote at length admonishing husbands to listen to their wives. It was actually one of my most read essays, and from time to time, my wife would remind me how popular it was even with her.

I found myself revisiting that passage about ten years later. The first thing that came to mind was that a man—husband, longtime boyfriend, or fiancé—must first have an open mind and a receptive heart in order to regard any words from the woman— wife, longtime girlfriend, fiancée, or even daughter(s)—in his life. But for the sake of simplicity let's presume she's his wife.

There must also be a measure of humility and integrity within the man, as well as a disposition to be a good man toward his woman. He must also recognize whether his choice of woman is one who has his best interests at heart, or she's nothing more than an opportunist. The former is far more desirable because she will have more credibility whenever she does speak. There are examples of the latter in the Bible where men listened to their wives at their own peril. They were wicked people who had wicked intentions and they reaped the consequences for it.

There must also be a measure of humility and integrity within the man, as well as a disposition to be a good man toward his woman.

Admittedly, I have allowed myself to complicate certain life situations by listening to the wrong source. There were times that I gave more credence to things suggested by individuals who did not have my best interests at heart, and in the end, I've at times had to literally pay for making the wrong decisions. There were also times that I did not regard things suggested by the few women who did have my best interests at heart and I regretted that I did not take them more seriously. Of course, there were the times when I regarded things suggested by those same few women who had my best interests at heart; things did work out. What I've found to be true back in 1999, and even now, there is a mindset that exists among men that if he listens to a woman it might be construed as a sign of weakness. His reaction may also be one of outright rebellion because it might remind him of being raised by his mother once again.

Men should not be looking for another mother. But what men should understand in its truest concept a relationship between a husband and wife should be one where the two parties complement each other. There will be times that the man does not have all the answers. The problems and/or situations that require his leadership in finding a solution may or may not have been borne by him. And in those scenarios the woman may have a broader view, offering a unique insight to get them through it. It could also be said that sometimes it takes an outside, impartial observer to apprise the man of the resource that he already had in his life by imploring him to listen to that woman.

In its truest concept a relationship between man and woman should be one where the two parties complement each other.

I've also found it to be true then, and even now, that a woman can become quite persistent and passionate in making her suggestions known to a man. Men are inclined to call it nagging, but there are times when a woman feels it is necessary that her man should listen to her. It could also be a sign of her frustration that he's not attending to her needs when the truth is that listening to her is one of her needs.

A woman wants to know within that relationship that she is the center of her man's attention and universe and that she's respected, valued, and cherished just as she was told when he was in pursuit of a relationship with her—or as she was taught to believe the way men should treat her.

Out of frustration, she'll go as far as trying to arrest his attention by making mention of other positive male examples in the way they regard the woman in their lives. If that doesn't work, she'll become turned off. Sometimes she'll let the man know. Other times she won't tell him. But there's a likelihood the man will go along thinking that everything is fine until it's reached a boiling point within the woman. It is unfortunate that may be the only time that the man even recognizes that he has a major problem to contend with in her dissatisfaction.

By then, the woman could have reached a point of detachment to the extent that she's already considered leaving the relationship. Then the man's reduced to asking, "Why didn't you tell me?"

Her response: "You never listened to me!"

Why find out when she's on her way out of the door? And why let her be left with intimating this to another man who's more than willing to listen to the very things that you failed to do?

IN REVIEW:

- There is the mindset that men should not listen to women because if they do it is a sign of obvious weakness.

- A husband should realize that his wife is to complement him just as he is to complement her, meaning that what she has to say does have importance.

- Sometimes a wife's nagging is her way of trying to get her husband's attention that something is wrong and it needs to be addressed.

- What happens when a husband fails to listen to his wife? Keep reading along.

An Introduction to the Communication Process

Alluding to my formal background in print journalism, a good reporter is able to craft an entire story around a single, notable quote even if the supporting facts and/or events for the story are horrible. Other times, the quote itself is what drives the story.

One of the more memorable quotes that I've shared with people comes from when I worked at my first daily newspaper following graduation from Texas Southern University. I was assigned to do a story for the *New Braunfels Herald-Zeitung*, which was located about a half-hour east of San Antonio, on a local guy who was an avid sportsman. There was talk of him becoming one of the on-air talents for the revival of the original *American Sportsman* series that was once famously hosted by sports broadcasting legend Curt Gowdy.

During my conversation with the local guy and the project's producer, the producer casually surmised, "It's about people, places, and communication." I understood that the airing of this show merely used *people* to *communicate* a message about hunting and sport while traveling to *places* and sharing these opportunities to others via a medium known as broadcast television. I've also recognized how that producer's comment has had relevance in simple every day living: It's always been about people, the places we've gone and aspire to go, and communication is the process by which we enlighten others about our journey.

I also was taught by Bob Giles, one of my instructors at TSU, being a good listener was one of the top traits he listed for a good journalist. (For the inquiring minds, the other attributes were an avid reader, love of people, openness, objectivity, sensitivity, organized, keen observer, faith/ confidence [in a higher being], and a good interviewer.)

I can't say that I always had a great love of people, or for that matter I was an avid reader of anything that did not involve sports. Nor could I say that I was always the most sensitive person in that I truly understood the plight of the individuals that I interviewed, or that I had any measure of empathy for them. I knew that I was always well prepared and organized. That was something another instructor of mine, Sam Andrews, indoctrinated in me after countless hours of conversation. But a noted exception was one of the first stories I worked on for a newspaper in Boca Raton, Florida. I did not realize until after a ninety-minute session with a golfing legend that there were no batteries in my recorder.

Embarrassing moment aside, I can still say that a good listener was paramount in my former profession. How could I ever ask questions that might yield a gold mine of information out of the person that I interviewed without developing the skill to listen? If I was the one doing all of the talking then I might as well have handed my tape recorder and notepad over to my interviewee and let him or her ask me the questions.

Among sports reporters, we often dealt with personalities with humongous egos, and it could be amusing at times knowing that some of them just loved to hear themselves talk. An axiom that I derived from that was many of them just wanted somebody to *listen* to them. Thus, one of my tricks of the trade that I employed was getting the other person into the interview by getting them to talk about themselves. The benefit was when I earned their trust they shared information with me that they may not have shared with other reporters.

Now one might assume that the acquired skill of listening should have easily transferred into many of my personal relationships. Not exactly. I may have used the attribute, or appearance thereof, to smoke-and-mirror my way into some interactions with women that resulted in selfish motives achieved. But when it came to a serious and committed relationship, the attribute was not as easily identifiable.

It might be said, too, that I've always had a knack for talking. Some might even say that I've always been perceived as an articulate guy who can converse on a wide range of topics. Inherently, some women may have found that quite appealing in me. What they did not immediately recognize was a great deal of shallowness within me. For that matter, if I had dared to listen to them, I might have spared myself of a lot of grief of indulging in women who were just as shallow that I had no business being around. But that's another conversation—for now.

According to Webster's *New Encyclopedic Dictionary*, communication is defined as an act or instance of transmitting; information communicated (a message), or an exchange of information. Another common definition is an imparting or interchange of thoughts, opinion, or information; understanding is the goal of all communication.

Communication works best when there is a flow of interaction, reaction and interaction, and there is an understanding derived from it. Somewhere in this is process is the ability to listen. Now some may say there is an art to listening. There may be some truth to that. I'll just say that it can become something acquired, so long as the person is willing to work at it.

Communication works best when there is a flow of interaction, reaction and interaction, and there is an understanding derived from it. Somewhere in this is process is the ability to listen.

The beauty of communication is that, by nature, humans are expressive beings. We ultimately crave and thrive for interaction with another person. How many times have you been so enraptured by a conversation with another person and you lose track of time?

Thus, that is why we seek companionship, and in some cases a lifelong companionship with someone. Admittedly, my wife is turned on by significant, weighty conversations with me, and likewise I'm also turned on by similar conversations with her.

Another appreciable aspect of communication is that we're not limited to one person doing the talking and the other person just listening. The communication process, when properly employed, allows us to take on interchangeable roles that can be equally impressive.

I was introduced to what is known as the Shannon-Weaver communications model during my first semester (Fall 1985) at

TSU. My instructor for this Communications 101 class was Ron Lomas. Of all the things that were covered in that class, the only lecture that I ever had any recollection of was the one where Lomas explained the Shannon-Weaver model by employing a couple of funny illustrations. But here's a tried and proven life lesson that I've learned: Nothing is ever wasted. It's never cease to amaze me the times that I've been able to draw upon experiences of having met someone, or having participated in something, and make application of it.

The Shannon-Weaver model is regarded as the most widely accepted format for interpersonal communication. Claude Shannon, a research mathematician for Bell Laboratories, is credited as being the father of information theory. His essay *A Mathematical Theory of Communication* (1949) explained how to maximize transmitting information that could be easily understood and interpreted with the least amount of distortion. It was intended solely for the use of telephones.

Years later, fellow scientist and mathematician Warren Weaver applied Shannon's mathematical concept to interpersonal communication and added the concept of feedback to the model. Shannon and Weaver co-authored a book titled *The Mathematical Theory of Communication* (1963). Much of the book's content is a reprint of Shannon's 1949 essay.

There are eight elements within the Shannon-Weaver model that can be applied to any means of transmitting a message (i.e., electronic, verbal, phone, written, texting): there is a source (sender), encoder, message, channel, noise, decoder, receiver, and feedback.

IN REVIEW:

- Communication is information that is communicated (a message) or an exchange of information.
- Communication works best when there is a flow of interaction, reaction, and interaction.
- The Shannon-Weaver model is the most widely accepted for interpersonal communication.

The Sender (encodes) and the Receiver (decodes)

In the previous chapter, I mentioned that communication works best when there is interaction, reaction and interaction, and there is an understanding derived from it. Somewhere in the process is the ability to listen. I feel the best way to explain this is by incorporating the Shannon-Weaver model into this discussion and its application as to why husbands should listen to their wives.

The **sender** is widely regarded as the one who initiates the interaction by transmitting his or her thoughts, opinion, or information in a way that a **receiver** can understand it. The receiver's role is to interpret the sender's thoughts, opinion, or information. He or she completes the process by providing interaction.

It is widely agreed upon that marriage is a two-way relationship. One gives, the other receives; one has needs that the other tries to meet, and likewise. The bond to their relationship is love, consideration, respect, patience, and faithfulness. No marriage can succeed when one party is giving its all while the other is merely a ravenous consumer or taker.

Communication is similarly a two-way process, and the parties who participate in it serve dual roles. Once the husband (or wife) has transmitted the initial message, he or she becomes the receiver of the message that's been transmitted by the other spouse. Ideally, this should be done willfully by both, because it is my opinion that effective communication within a marriage produces unity and selflessness.

Using the communication process model, when a wife complains that her husband never listens to her it's because she's determined that he's consistently failed to participate as a receiver of her messages. Simply put, he's ignored her, he's chosen to tune out whenever it's convenient for him, or he's failed to respond or act upon anything she says to him.

Marriage is a two-way relationship. Communication is similarly a two-way process, and the parties who participate in it serve dual roles.

Another scenario might be when the husband is known to react to his wife's attempts at communicating with an assortment of histrionics and finding fault with her for the most mundane of reasons. What is unfortunate is that an argument is likely to ensue because either or both parties feel like the other person is wasting their time. And if there are any insults or threats in the exchange, both feel it is necessary to protect themselves from any damaging words, acts, or gestures.

Both spouses come across as what I'll describe as dueling senders because they're talking at each other and their words are like rattling swords. At some point those words will prick and pierce into one's heart and psyche for all the wrong reasons. As a result, nothing is accomplished. Nobody's listened. Understanding was not achieved; that's not communication nor is it building up a marriage.

Sheri and Bob Stritof, marriage counselors and regular contributors to About.com's Guide to Marriage, once wrote, "When one or both of you are not listening to one another, you have a problem in your marriage. If the lack of listening continues, your marriage could be in jeopardy."

These days, I'm deeply saddened whenever I'm apprised of marital situations that have reached a crisis point because I know what it's like to have sent my wife to despair because of my unwillingness to treat my marriage as a two-way street as opposed to a dead end.

Sometimes she would warn me of some of the mistakes other husbands have made with their wives. On one particular occasion, she mentioned to me about a husband who had always maintained a job, but for years he got high, drunk, spent his time in porn and he frequented strip joints. His father lived a similar lifestyle as well as several other men in his family. His parents separated before he reached adolescence. The wife, whose parents were school administrators and were still married after forty-five years, worked various jobs. They also struggled financially year after year. They had two children who were elementary and middle school age, respectively.

According to the wife's account, the husband had never listened to her about changing his lifestyle. He complained that she was trying to become his mother. That was usually cause for an argument, or even a fight that ended with the husband storming out of the house and not returning for days. The wife surprised him after one of those arguments by changing the locks and having him served a restraining order. The couple is now divorced—much to the satisfaction of her parents who had advised her not to marry him in the first place.

"Can't you see that their lives could have been much better had he just treated his wife with respect?" my wife attempted to reason with me.

"So what?" I remember hissing at her. "That's him, not me!"

"You're right. It isn't you, but it could become you because you refuse to change the way that you treat this marriage. We don't need to head down that path."

What my wife tried to reason with me was that a woman can only take so much hurt and disappointment before she resorts to something drastic. It was described to me that the woman's family hired a divorce attorney for her and presented a case that portrayed the husband as a terror and a lunatic. The judge asked the husband if he had done anything to improve their marriage. The husband attempted to point out faults about the wife, but the judge abruptly decided to award the wife the cars, the house, and both alimony and child support.

"That could have been avoided had he just listened to his wife and straighten up his life," my wife said. "There was so much potential in him."

"Yeah, right," I scoffed. "The judge only saw how much potential in making his life miserable until the day he dies."

That exchange resulted in a horrible argument for us. It was several weeks before we attempted to resolve our differences. Whatever sex we had at that time was perfunctory at best. And in my moments of reflection from that era, I'll identify myself as a dueling source and an unwilling receiver because I was still headstrong about doing things my way, which included mocking and ignoring my wife at every opportunity.

Encoding and Decoding

Let's establish that men and women communicate and interpret messages differently. When I worked in sales, I recall watching a video that suggested various words that we should use to reach men and women in the sales process. For example, when making a qualitative product comparison, we were instructed to use words like "feel," "think," and "know" with women so that we could appeal to their emotions since many of their buying decisions are based on that premise.

Conversely, I had better success with male customers when I centered my sales effort on conveying a high degree of competence while I explained the technical aspects of the products that I sold, and then giving them the bottom line. That's because most men make buying decisions based on logic. If it were a husband-and-wife combination, I focused most of my attention on the wife because I knew that she had the greatest influence in the buying process.

Let's also establish that women are more expressive when it comes to interpersonal communication. Women crave for meaningful dialogue so that they can share their thoughts and emotions with whom they relate to. The latter is what meets their propensity for bonding. Where as, men are less expressive in most modes of communication, and if there is any expressions conveyed it is likely to be done physically as in sex or some form of competition.

Using the three C's of journalism, it is my opinion that men will generally communicate and respond to messages being clear, concise, and correct—with an emphasis on clarity and conciseness. "As long as it is kept short we'll listen and hear," said a male respondent within my social network of more than 16,000 contacts. "It's when they start rambling that we start to tune you out."

Men may think of a woman's message as one that will *convict* them of something wrong, or it's an attempt at *conforming* them into their likeness and disposition. Very little of what they say has any *comfort* to them. It's something like the three C's of the Holy Spirit that I learned many years ago, but with women it's more of an emphasis on the convicting and conforming parts. And whenever a man tries providing feedback to them, nothing he says is correct, nor what he says ever really makes any sense and what he says is perceived as never to the point.

So how do men reach a happy medium when one considers these differences? The rule of thumb is that there must be a value placed on the exchange of information, opinions, and thoughts by both spouses. Otherwise, you've just given your spouse a leading excuse as to why you've tuned out without even a chance at attaining any understanding to any message transmitted.

In their online article "When Your Spouse Won't Listen," the Stritofs compared marriages as two people in adjacent hotel suites. "Openness in a marriage is keeping both doors open all the time," they wrote. "This type of openness comes from a willingness to share from one's heart.

"If your partner closes the door to his/her room, you can't open it. Only the person in the other room can open the door."

Now, how many times has a wife complained about not being able to talk to her husband in terms that he can understand, and vice versa? And how many times has a husband complained about not being able to understand anything his wife is communicating to him, and vice versa?

A woman's complaint might be that she can't understand grunts and eye movements. She needs words and plenty of them spoken. It is imperative that he understands and gives her feedback about what she's communicating to him; otherwise, that's a recipe for trouble.

"They say they're listening, but don't understand a damn thing they were just told," vented a female respondent from my social network.

And a man's complaint might be that he can't understand a woman's silence, ranting and raving, or her irresponsiveness during sex.

"When they pretend to listen, and when you look for feedback, they stutter," argued one male respondent.

For the sake of discussion, and according to the Shannon-Weaver model, the sender's role is to **encode** the information, thoughts, and/or actions that may comprise the intended message of words (either written or spoken) in such a way that the receiver can easily and effectively **decode** the message in terms that he or she can interpret and best understand. Sufficed to say, if all couples were capable and willing to do this, perhaps a significant portion of relational problems might be solved.

One of the biggest challenges that I've observed in many marriage relationships involved the ability or inability to structure messages that the other person might receive as well as the ability or inability to interpret the messages transmitted, and then offer useful feedback.

A few years back, my wife related to me a scenario that involved a couple that had been married for about twenty years. They had a son and daughter who were in high school. The wife was a lead registered nurse and the husband had business aspirations for about as long as they had been married. Both were heavily involved in church, although neither was in ministry.

As my wife explained to me, the woman had grown frustrated with her husband in all aspects of her marriage. She became so detached from him that she even faked orgasms for at least fifteen years out of their marriage, and if it weren't for the children she would have left her husband for another man.

"Some times a woman smiles to hide the pain that exists in her life," my wife told me. "She's hurting and she's hurting bad. The husband has no clue. No matter how she tries telling him, he just doesn't get it. I don't know how much more she's going to take of this."

It did not take long for me to tune out on my wife and launch a counterattack. "So what does this have to do with me?" I lashed out at her. "Why do you come to me with all these people?"

"Because maybe you might allow for something to make its way inside your thick head and you'll see that there are others out there who are going through what we're going through. Is that what you want for your marriage? Because you're not too far behind—"

"Well, that isn't me. And don't try comparing me to him!"

My wife persisted with the story because she knew that I also had business aspirations. She explained to me that the husband had been very optimistic with his business venture in the beginning. His ultimate goal was to help others become financially independent. He quoted Bible scripture and sayings from successful entrepreneurs. But whenever his wife suggested to him that he also needed to treat her with respect and not as a sex object, and that he needed to reconsider the quality of people whom he'd established business relationships with, he lashed out at her that she was nothing more than a cynic and a hater.

What the wife was concerned about was her husband had gone through more than $250,000—much of it money she'd given him—with little or no return on their investment over the past decade. A marketing consultant had bilked him for $50,000. And the husband invested more than $100,000 in two business locations that were not conducive to the products he wanted to sell.

"And guess what the wife told him?" my wife posed to me; I responded with a semi-blank stare. "At some point you're going to have to decide whether this is worth pursuing especially in this economy. There's a lot we could be doing with much of the money that's gone into your business dreams."

My wife went on to say that woman often voiced her frustration among others about her inability to get her message across to her husband. She eventually would scoff and sigh, "I can stand in front of him with flashing signs and thunder and lighting from above, and it still won't make a difference with him."

I once heard a minister tell his congregation that men have to be allowed the opportunity to fail, but he also questioned at what cost?

It was apparent that whenever the wife tried communicating with her husband that she could not effectively encode her message. Nor could the husband decode it in a way that he might heed her advice and without any confrontation. Having gone through $250,000 should have been enough of a message encoded to alert her husband that maybe it hadn't worked.

Ah, but wives out of their propensity to bond and keep family units together are so longsuffering. So many times, they'll pray for that wayward husband who refuses to admit that he's too stubborn to change or take heed to sound wisdom. That is so honorable and godly; I know that I'm a result of it. But along the way, when she's not seeing any results, she'll probably ask herself what will it take before he listens? In addition, when will he be capable of making decisions that would be in the best interests of that relationship?

"Bottom line, there's nothing you can do to get your spouse to listen, if he or she doesn't want to listen," the Stritofs said.

However, here are some steps to consider:

- Suggest a weekly meeting.

- Ask how often you would like to meet. And both of you agree on the frequency.

- Create the right mood or setting.

- Ask how can we improve your communication?

- Ask how would you rate your relationship?

- Talk on terms that both can understand and provide positive feedback (and not negative).

- Don't rush to judge or find fault.

Some lack maturity and wisdom to consider or value solid advice. Sadly, in some life situations, it takes something more drastic before a person finally gets it. It's usually in the form of a great loss—divorce, financial ruin, or even death—before some finally understand what others have been trying to say.

Such was the case with another couple my wife related to me. The couple lived in South Carolina, where my wife was born and raised, and they were married for more than thirty years at the time of the husband's death. He was a man of medium stature and his trade was specialty woodworks. He met his wife not long after a stint in the military. They had three children, all of whom went on to earn college diplomas, but they struggled financially from year to year.

"The first time he ever really considered anything his wife told him was a year before his death," she told me. "That was when he was diagnosed with cancer. Even then, his wife had told him for years to visit a doctor, but he told her that there was nothing wrong with him."

My wife went on to describe that the husband and wife were never known for any outward displays of affection. Over the years the wife and husband became detached from each other, and the only reason why they never divorced was because their marriage was the only lifestyle that they knew.

What further complicated the marriage was that the husband was known to have had numerous adulterous relationships and he drank. Whenever the wife went to church, he'd mock her. "Make sure you tell Jesus that I said, 'Hey.' Do that now, you hear?"

It was not until the husband had progressed to an advanced stage of cancer before he ever considered changing any aspect of his life. All of a sudden, he was in church every Sunday. He apologized to his wife for many of his mistakes during their marriage. He was appreciative of her staying with him to the end when she could have deserted him. "Two months before he died, I'm told that he even kissed his wife before he left for the doctor," my wife added. "That was never heard of."

My wife described that the husband died of cancer, but his death was also attributed to an accident. According to my wife, the husband was very sick and could barely walk. The wife told him that she was going to the store, which was about a half-hour roundtrip from where they lived. The last thing she said to him before leaving was to stay in bed.

When the wife returned home, a trail of blood was discovered from the bathroom back to the bedroom where the husband convalesced. The husband had fallen and hit his head on the bathroom sink. Before he slipped into a coma and died his last words to his wife were, "You were right. I should have listened... I'm sorry."

How simple of a message was encoded? Stay in bed. Sadly, some of us still have an inability to decode declarative statements like that even unto death.

IN REVIEW:

- Marriage should be viewed as a two-way street or process, and the communication process is similar in that the parties who participate serve dual roles.

- According to the Shannon-Weaver model for communication, the sender encodes a message. And the person who is the receiver decodes a message.

- Encoding involves the sender transmitting a message in ways the receiver might be best able to understand. Decoding involves the receiver interpreting the message in ways that he or she might be best able to understand.

The Message: 'The Things We Say and Do Not Say'

A **message** is the information, thought and/or action that is to be transmitted by the sender and/or receiver. It's like the tennis ball that travels from one side of the court to the other during a match.

The Shannon-Weaver model did not allow for the quality or significance of a message's content. It was only concerned about a message being received with reciprocating feedback to fuel the communication process.

Along those lines, the message a person transmits may be something that helps us to decide whether an individual might have relevance with us. But someone forgot to remind me of that not long after I met my wife in the fall of 1993. One of my more embarrassing moments occurred when I lost connection with her during a phone conversation only to find out years later that she had become so disgusted that she pulled the phone chord.

I don't know if I should be credited with being persistent,

but I had the nerve to call her back thinking that maybe I had done something with my phone. More than likely, I was off into another discourse about myself. And for all I know, it could have pertained to me talking about the ninety-minute commute that I made several times a week while I covered the University of South Carolina's athletic program, or it could have been about some of the places that I had traveled to at that point in my career.

"You know I've always been one about talking with substance," she eventually explained to me. "My father was one who watched and listened. He didn't talk much. So when he did say something it really meant something."

Apparently, when my wife decided to pull the phone chord on me, she essentially told me that nothing I said had any relevance. Yet I've always been able to laugh at what my wife did to me that evening; it was a difficult lesson learned.

In other areas of life, we hear the term "message" being associated with ministers and politicians. Taking the latter as an example, a candidate may be most remembered or judged for it.

I recall back in 2004 when my wife asked me about some guy named Barack Obama because she was impressed with his keynote speech at the Democratic National Convention that year in Boston.

"Oh, yeah," I answered. "He's the one who's running for senator in Illinois. There's a good chance that he will be elected. He'll be the first black since Carol Mosley Braun, who won her race in 1990."

"Let me tell you," she said, "he's going places."

Even when Obama announced he was running for president in early 2007, I did not think much of it again until South Carolina's

Democratic Party primary a year later. It was only then when I heard his *message* for the first time that I realized that he had something that I could identify with and it made him tangible to me. I began following him much closer as the 2008 presidential campaign progressed. He proved to be a worthy candidate.

I later learned that, yes, even President Obama understands the importance of listening to his wife, Michelle. According to a published media report in the *New York Daily News,* it noted that Obama was skeptical about his now famous "Yes We Can" campaign slogan that was suggested by his advisor, David Axelrod, during his run for the U.S. Senate.

The article mentioned Obama went as far as to say, as it was published in *Barack and Michelle: Portrait of an American Marriage* (by Christopher Andersen), that Axelrod's idea was corny and childish, and he asked other members of his campaign staff to come up with a better slogan. Mrs. Obama, however, thought it was a good idea and convinced her husband to go along with it.

Shall we say the rest is history?

'The Things We Say...'

From time to time, I've been made aware of the saying *it's not what you say; it's how you say it that makes all the difference in the world.* The message that we transmit—verbally or non-verbally—has resonance with the people we interact with, and its impact can be both positive and negative.

It is my understanding from years of Bible study that it doesn't really teach us specifically what to say to our spouses, but it does teach us how we are to conduct ourselves around them. My wife is a big proponent of the Bible-based teaching that we are known by the fruit that is produced from our lives. Therefore, our words should follow suit, for it is a reflection of what is really inside us.

Jesus went as far as to say, "For out of the abundance of the heart the mouth speaks...But I say to you that for every idle word men may speak, they will give an account of it in the day of judgment. For by your words you will be justified, and by your words you will be condemned." (Matthew 12:34, 36-27)

The message that we transmit can also affect whether the other person will listen or not. What I'm about to say is not qualified by empirical data, yet it is my opinion based on personal experience and observation that some men do not listen to their wives and/or they tune out on their wives because of the way they communicate to them.

The message that we transmit can also affect whether the other person will listen or not.

If the wife's message is full of complaints, nagging, and berating, it is likely the husband's self worth is being attacked and his non-listening is a sign of preserving it. I have heard one minister say that a man responds to a woman who respects him—the Bible exhorts a wife to respect her husband.

If the wife is taking too long to say what she wants to say, the husband is likely to tune out. If she has a tendency to dominate the conversations, he's likely to shut down on her. If she's demeaning and derogatory, he'll take exception to that. If it seems that all she does is preach and lecture to him, and there is no opportunity for him to participate in the process, he's likely to both shut down and tune out. If she continues to bring up the same old thing, over and over again, he's likely to tell her to find something else to talk about. Meanwhile, he's going to walk out of the room and find a place of refuge from her, much to her dissatisfaction. If she has a tendency to make sweeping statements that he never does anything, or that he constantly fails at everything, at some point he's going to become equally insulting and demeaning.

Connie Grigsby, who co-authored *How to Get Your Husband to Listen to You,* compared respect being the lifeblood for a man as being loved, honored, and cherished is to a woman. According to God's design, Christ is the head of His bride, the church, just as the man is recognized as the head of the family unit. Therefore, respect is due to him simply because of his position, she said.

The Bible declares that a woman's respect for her husband should be as unto the Lord himself.

"I think women struggle with this because they feel like their husbands need to earn this respect...So we need to stop thinking our husband has to earn it. We need to start thinking just the very nature of the role they fulfill, which is husband, demands my respect," she said in a Christian Broadcasting Network (CBN) article.

At the time their book *Up, Up and Away: How We Found Love, Faith, and Lasting Marriage in the Entertainment World* was published, music legends Marilyn McCoo and Billy Davis, Jr., formerly of the 5th Dimension, were celebrating their 35th wedding anniversary.

Ms. McCoo and Mr. Davis said that their marriage has had its peaks and valleys despite the public's perception of one that's been rock solid the entire time. The peaks have included Grammy award winning songs and albums with the 5th Dimension and then when they ventured on their own to perform as a duet;

Marilyn accepted salvation in 1981 and Billy recommitted himself to the Lord a few months later; and Billy overcame both alcoholism and prostate cancer. The valleys have included marital difficulties brought about by Billy's drinking and then them simply not knowing how to communicate with each other. It was so bad that during the mid-1970s, at the peak of their musical popularity, that they sought counseling.

In those early years of their marriage, Marilyn felt it was necessary to correct Billy both privately and publicly for things he said and did around her whenever he didn't measure up to her standards.

"[It] had been ingrained into me at a very young age...this perfectionistic streak ran in my family," she wrote.

"My stubborn perfectionism followed me into my adult life and impacted on how I interacted with those who knew me well."

The counseling sessions revealed that Marilyn's perfectionism prevented her from not regarding what Billy desired to communicate to her. "At times, I felt that Marilyn wasn't listening to me because she thought I had been drinking or had nothing to say," he wrote. "When she listened to me, everything went fine." He went on to relate that he wanted to see more of that from Marilyn.

Billy also admitted that he did not have the patience to listen to Marilyn because she ranted and nagged excessively. "When she sounded like a broken record, I just turned her off," he wrote. "When she accused me of shutting down, she was right."

He said he later realized when he tuned out on her there were occasions when he may have missed out on something that could have benefitted both of them. This newfound respect for Marilyn's input enabled Billy to value her in a way that the Bible exhorts a husband to love his wife—and dwell with her with understanding—because it brought growth to their relationship.

"If we don't do that for one another, we're missing out on the best part of the relationship, which is communication from the heart," he said. "Now I look forward to what she has to say."

Toward the end of the book, Marilyn said the Lord had impressed upon her that she could improve herself by not being such a perfectionist. She felt that shedding that trait could help her become a better wife toward Billy.

"Our marriage improved immensely when this happened," she wrote. "The marital spats dwindled to a trickle."

It is estimated that forty percent of all men have had at least one affair in their current marital relationship. Overall, about sixty percent of all men will admit to cheating on their partner.

Generally speaking, the lack of respect that some wives give their husbands is a common excuse and reason why some men admit to venturing off into an extramarital affair. Similar reasons include having too many arguments, or dealing with an overly critical spouse.

Has this not been said before? "She makes me feel like a man." Quite possibly, the woman whom he's drifted off with could very well be willing to treat him in a way that he's not receiving from his wife. This does not justify an affair, because many are products of selfishness and lust, but it may be a factor that leads to one.

Of course, I've heard some women react, "Well, if he ever treated me with respect, he just might find that he'll get respect."

They're right. But I'm going to question that attitude because there are some women who are a product of the environment from where they were raised. In other words, if a young girl has seen other women consistently curse, berate and yell at a man, and there is no rationale for it, she might presume that is the correct way to treat a man when she's involved with one.

True story: I'm reminded of a woman whom I was involved with. She often yelled when she talked to me, and at times she berated me. When I saw how her mother interacted with others, it became clearly obvious to me where it came from. Therefore, it is very important as parents that we set the right example for our children.

My daughter constantly reminds me of that especially when I apprise her of less-than-desirable behavior. She says, "In case you've forgotten, I'm just like you, dad. Where do you think I get it from?" And she's right.

Conversely, the same thing could be said about a young man who has only seen men cursing, yelling, and berating women. When the woman implores the man not to treat her that way, there is the likelihood that he will ignore her because he's a product of his environment.

Sadly, some husbands refuse to listen to their wives as an attempt at showing who's in control of the relationship. Making the woman genuflect to his will is an overt way of assuaging his already fractured ego. This lack of honor is exacerbated from generation to generation.

I was intrigued by a marital situation in which the couple had been together for more than twenty-five years. They had an adult child who's now in his early twenties. The wife said after all their years together that she had become accustomed to her husband not listening to her nor considering anything she had to say.

Determined to press on with her life, she said, "I've had to pick and choose my fights with what I've had to say [to him].

And you know what? I'm like this: If you don't listen to me, I'm not going to stress myself out that you're not listening to me."

She went on to say that she had researched material on ways to communicate more effectively with her husband. Some of it suggested that she should change the way her message was being transmitted to him. Try talking in a calm, collected tone. Set a pleasant environment for her conversation. Compliment him for the things that he has done right.

"I've tried talking to him," she said, sighing. "But he still doesn't listen at all. He hears all the bitching, moaning, and complaining. It still doesn't get to him."

It is unfortunate that not every couple will improve their marriage. Some of them merely mask their problems through money, trips, gifts, and even absolute autonomy, but the underlying issues still persist. This is what the wife of more than twenty-five years has reluctantly accepted.

"Rather than listening to me, he'd rather pacify me with the freedom to do what I want, money to do what I want, or he'll accommodate me with a great car," she said. "But I feel he does those things just to pacify me."

'... The Things We Do Not Say'

It is estimated that between fifty and eighty percent of all human communication is non-verbal, and it is generally comprised by four categories:

- Physical: It includes facial expressions, vocal inflections and tone, touch, smell and other body motions.

- Aesthetic: Communication that takes place through creative expressions like dancing, painting, sculpturing, and playing musical instruments.

- Signs: Flags, horns, and sirens.

- Symbolic: Use of religious, status, or ego-building symbols (like cars, bodybuilding, clothes, and money)

Other facets of non-verbal communication include our behavior, the proximity from which we interact with others, and the gestures that we make. They are also interchangeable and the communication can be intentional or unintentional.

Noted psychologists Judith Hall and Mark Knapp surmised that we constantly transmit messages about our attitudes, feelings, and personality; and those who receive our messages might become skillful at decoding and interpreting them.

Albert Mehrabian, a psychology professor, is widely credited with determining that there are three basic elements in any face-to-face communication: visual, verbal, and vocal.

Through his work, Mehrabian is also credited with establishing the premise that people will believe more of what they see than what is said in situations of face-to-face communication, and that the attitudes and feelings that pertain to a message is mostly derived from the way the message was said and in the person's facial expressions.

His research, which was conducted during the 1960s, was based on positive and/or negative reactions to single words spoken and not a string of words spoken in situations of face-to-face communication; he suggested that this was true about ninety-three percent of the time. Factors that could affect the percentage included how well the receiver knew the sender of the message, other body language, and the context of what was communicated.

In the academic arena, non-verbal communication has a significant effect on the learning process in children, notes

Frederick Douglas Boyd, Sr., whose doctoral dissertation was on this subject[1].

For example, Boyd determined among at-risk black males, who are subject to being lost between both societal and educational cracks because of poor academic performance and little or no educational support from home, the teachers who were most effective with them were those whose non-verbal behavior/ communication included interaction in closeness to them and an invasion of their space, changing their voice inflections to emphasize they were talking to them, and making eye contact[2].

Non-verbal communication is not only silence, but it's typically our behavior, body language and the gestures that we make

---

These students, ages eleven to fifteen in the study, were more receptive to instruction, and there was a marked increase in academic performance and a reduction in disciplinary referrals. The effective teachers were also those who listened to their students[3].

"More than any other aspect of communication," Boyd wrote, "the skill of listening is the least studied and the most taken for granted...The art of listening may be one of the teacher's most important assets. Listening is essential for thinking in the classroom and for appropriate response. Listen for feelings as well as facts."

When it comes to relationships, it is my opinion that women are far better at observing others than men, because men usually don't spend as much time dissecting the other person's words and how they were articulated, or studying non-verbal clues and giving feedback about them unless it pertains to something important to them or it's long after the fact. Men are likely to consider it as immaterial.

It would help if husbands learned a lesson or two about the things that go unspoken in a marriage. Many trips to marriage counselors or even divorce court could be averted if they paid attention to the non-verbal communication transmitted by their wives. This is why effective decoding is so essential. A similar thought would be that a spouse's non-verbal messages can be easily misinterpreted just as his or her verbal messages. They also can affect how spouses might trust one another, provoke an individual to be defensive, trigger withdrawal from a spouse, stall the communication process, and intensify hostility in a marriage.

For example, where as a woman's silence might be perceived as a warning sign for a man, his silence might be perceived as insulting and annoying with her. A woman not only wants to hear her man interact with her, she expects that he's actively engaged in the conversation.

So that means instead of him just saying "uh-huh, I'm listening..." while he's slouched in his chair, a woman tends to expect for the man to straighten up his posture, provide eye contact, and engage in meaningful feedback.

Says the wife, for example, "I don't feel that people really understand how I feel at the office. Everything seems to fall on my shoulders." She shifts where she's sitting and sighs. That may be a clue to the husband that he should sit closer to his wife because she's looking for assurance and agreement.

"I'm sure that your work does not go unnoticed. Maybe it was just a bad day today."

"No, you don't get it. This is every day."

"Alright, I see what you're saying. You're saying that people are taking advantage of you. They don't realize just how valuable you are."

"Yes, that's it. If I'm not there, that place is a zoo. Nothing gets done."

"Well you know what you're asking for: Respect. I'd tell them to pay you for your pain and suffering."

"You know, that's not a bad idea—"

Wives also interpret husbands not listening to them by their glassy-eyed reactions; the fidgeting, squirming, and shifting in seats; the crossing of arms, tilting of heads to the side and expressionless face; or the huffing that's made whenever she's alerted them that they need to talk.

How many times an exchange like this has occurred:

"You're not listening to me," she reacts to him glancing off to his right at the wall. "You never listen to me."

"I am listening to you."

"Then why don't you show me that you are?"

Annoyed, the husband points his finger in the wife's direction and he's glaring at her. "Look, I'm not a child. I'm a grown man. I can do whatever I please. And if I decide to listen to you standing on my head, I can do it." He straightens up in his seat. "Besides, I was just getting comfortable."

Now the wife rushes in front of him, places one hand on her waist, wags a finger at him, and rolls her neck while she responds. "You call that getting comfortable? I call that being disrespectful and insulting. I'm not going to put up with that."

The husband throws his hands up. "So what do you want me to do?"

"Never mind," she now huffs in disgust. "Just remember that when you want something from me. See how you'll take it when it happens to you."

The husband waves off his wife and walks out of the room, grumbling, "She must think that I'm her child or something. I'll show her."

Much of that heated interaction could have been diffused by the husband showing more attentiveness to his wife's attempt at communicating with him. He would have transmitted the message to her that he was respectful of her desire to engage in a conversation, and he was willing to provide her the necessary feedback.

Although there was not much else provided, this interaction could have occurred when the husband had just arrived home from work. Men tend to want time just to relax before they engage in any conversation. It is their way of coping with stress as they separate themselves from what had transpired during the workday.

A bit of patience and consideration by both parties could also have gone a long way. The wife could have helped herself out by inquiring whether it was a good time for her to discuss matters with him. Another thing she could have done was establish that she wanted for them to have a better understanding of what the discussion was about. She could have also chosen a different set of words to initiate the conversation. Since men are more task and solution oriented, she could have said, "I need your help with this . . ." or "I would like your input on something I've been thinking about . . ." Those words might be perceived as less confrontational.

A common complaint by many wives is that husbands don't give them quality attention. How many times have she's stood before a mirror beautifying herself, and when she emerges from her preparation she's smiling. She may do a pirouette and stop, inquiring to him, "Well, how do I look?"

The husband glances up—if he does at all—and offers little response. Maybe he might say, "You look alright." Then he asks her, "So when you're making dinner?" Or he might respond, "So when we're going to get it on because I'm in the mood."

That's likely to send the husband out to the doghouse because he failed to take time to appreciate her work. It will remain in the wife's memory bank until he apologizes to her for that, or he makes the effort to recognize her with sincerity and without any provocation.

Now the reason why the husband was in trouble is because had he'd been listening to his wife, he would have recognized her seeking approval in the way she prepared herself rather than him responding to her with questions that solely met his own needs or desires.

In that scenario, the wife may have tried something different in her marriage, and it could have very well been her intention to spark meaningful conversation with him. She not only wanted to spend time with him, but she wanted his undivided attention. This is something that often goes unnoticed by husbands.

In another scenario, the wife has planned on having a conversation with her husband. She's decided that she would articulate ways that he could show his appreciation for her: buying her a card other than for Mother's Day, wedding anniversary, or birthday; candy and/or flowers; take her out to lunch or dinner and later to a movie; or he could take time out to just talk with her to find out what's really going on with her rather than expecting for her to have sex with him just because he's in the mood.

"Even a simple 'I love you' could really go a long way with me," she mentions to him. "It tells me that you actually took the time out to say that you care."

"I do love you."

"You're only saying it after I've told you."

Eventually the verbal reminders cease. Now all the husband gets is silence. Silence is one of the major non-verbal communication messages transmitted in many relationships. When a wife becomes uncharacteristically silent, she's telling her husband that something's wrong, and he needs to address it in a proactive way. He should make it a priority to find out what is going on with his wife and attend to those needs.

Silence is one of the major non-verbal communication messages transmitted in many relationships.

Admittedly, I tried ignoring my wife's silence because I knew there would be an avalanche of pent-up emotions seeking release. And even when she unloaded on me, I still ignored it and waved her off as being a nag. The problem was that we were not making any progress because we were mired in the same old cycle of futility.

Now here's where husbands—especially those who profess to be a Christian—may feel like somebody's beating them over their heads with scripture. The Bible does say his prayers might be hindered if he fails to love his wife, dwell with her with understanding, and treat her as though the weaker vessel.

Others might feel helpless and have no choice. Or as one lady from my social network quipped, "Yeah, because he knows I will raise hell. Then I'll ask him what I was talking about!"

On more than an occasion or two, I have been reminded by my wife about those little things that I could initiate to alleviate a major crisis. These were things that could not be done every once in a while. They had to be done consistently. I decided it was time for me to become not only a hearer of her words, but also a doer of them.

"I'm not that hard to please," she said. "You just need to realize what a difference it will make if you ever decide to do the things that will make your marriage better."

The Bible describes the joining of a man and woman in matrimony like a mystery, yet it is akin to Christ's relationship with the church. (Ephesians 5:32) And the wife is to carry herself in such a way that the beauty of the inner person is revealed to her husband rather than the outer person. Both of these truths can be confusing to a husband who has no understanding of either one.

My wife was the first one to articulate during our marriage that men and women are inherently different. We have different wants and desires in addition to the way we express ourselves. In recent years, for example, I've come to understand that when a woman encodes her message to a man there are more non-verbal messages transmitted. Women are likely to hint at men what they are truly communicating and it's up to the men to decode that message—or as my wife says, "Figure it out for yourself."

According to communication experts when women converse among each other they are adept at filling in those blanks. They're likely to finish off each other's sentences in anticipation of what the other person is going to say. This is a part of their bonding and understanding of each other where as a man might interpret that as somebody being a know-it-all and threatening.

So let's use a common household scenario of the wife wishing that the husband might help with washing the dishes. She just returned from the store and notices her husband is sitting where she left him—in front of a television—and making matters worse he did not even bother to help with bringing in the many bags of groceries.

On this particular occasion, she says, "You know it would be nice if you noticed some of the things that might need to be done around the house—"

"Huh?"

Let's say the wife did not respond, but she went ahead with putting up the groceries and washing the dishes. But there's a good chance that eventually the wife will not be as considerate of his feelings and she'll just vent her frustration.

Perhaps on another occasion if he fails to offer any help or take the initiative with washing the dishes, she might complain, "You know what? You never do anything around the house. You expect for me to clean, cook, sew, iron, wash the dishes, and then be ready and willing to be in the mood when you're in the mood...You need to take my feelings into consideration!"

"Why didn't you say you wanted me to help with washing the dishes? You know I'd help out."

"I've been telling you that all along. Every time I've come back from the store or work and I see a sink full of dishes. You could really be a blessing to me by doing that, but you're not."

In a scenario like that, early in our marriage my wife would have said that I should have known what she was really telling me; however, my response would be more along the lines of I'm not a mind reader.

"But if you were really into me then you would understand these things," she'd reply.

Then I would retort, "I still don't get it."

"I know. At least you're honest."

The mere fact that she would say that if *I were really into her* was a trigger phrase for me to tune out on her. I felt that I did not have to go through so many hoops and rings, so to speak, in order to understand her. I often grumbled to myself that the problem wasn't me; it was her.

The best thing that a husband can do is to become proactive and ask his wife questions whenever he does not understand what she's communicating to him. It's not a difficult thing to do, but men's egos have a way of getting in the way of doing something that could be of benefit to their marriage. A wife is likely to appreciate the fact that the husband is making the effort at understanding her. That's the type of investment that can produce a rather profitable return.

IN REVIEW:

- A **message** is the information, thought and/or action that is to be transmitted by the sender and/or receiver.

- We usually transmit a message either verbal or non-verbal.

- Non-verbal communication involves silence, gestures, behavior, and body language.

- We constantly transmit messages about our attitudes, feelings, and personality; and those who receive our messages might become skillful at decoding and interpreting them.

Noise, Noise, and More Noise . . .

It might be fair at this point for me to define, in my opinion, what does it mean for a husband to listen to his wife. Based on the many examples I've already given, as well as personal experience, it is a husband's willfulness to regard and act upon thoughts, opinion, and information from his wife based on the understanding that she has his best interests at heart. It does not mean he's become subservient to his wife, but he is mindful that his wife is an equal partner in their marriage.

Now I don't want to be viewed as making any excuses for a husband who does not listen to his wife. My goal in this chapter is to identify the many factors that can interfere and distort any message that's transmitted based on the Shannon-Weaver communication model.

Communication experts summarize this as **noise**. The Shannon-Weaver model asserts that the communication process is affected by the mode the message is to be transmitted, how accurately the message is transmitted, and how effective does the message received affects behavior.

Clearly to a wife, whenever her husband fails to regard what she says to him, the effect must have been negative. Thus, it is not surprising to hear one wife complain, "My spouse is the only male I've ever known who does NOT listen to me. Even when I give a very short and specific answer, he doesn't listen. I've been married for 21 years and he has NO idea what my favorite flower is, what I like to eat, what I like to do as a hobby, what my favorite movie is, or favorite color. Totally, no clue!"

In the interest of fair disclosure, there's been a lot of embedded noise between my ears that has prevented me from listening to my wife or anybody for that matter. There was also a point in my marriage when I was not far behind that woman's assessment of her husband. The only thing that distinguished me from the above-mentioned was that I knew of my wife's favorite color(s), and I had a working knowledge of what was her favorite restaurant and dish. But I had no idea or any desire to learn of anything else about her.

I will venture to say that husbands themselves can easily distort the communication process when they're already disengaged from their marriage, so nothing that wives say really matters to them. There are some who don't ostensibly frustrate the wife by their inability to listen to what she's saying, but he absolutely drives her mad when he'll appear to be a willing and engaged participant in their dialogue – yet his subsequent actions are far from it. Some call it paying her lip service.

In a probable scenario, a wife urges her husband not to leave his bath towel on the bathroom door. She explains to him that she tries keeping a clean place. The least he could do is show some appreciation by placing the towel on one of the racks, or simply putting it in the hamper.

Initially embarrassed, he might say, "I understand exactly what you're saying, dear—"

"Do you really?" she replies, hoping it is true. "You know how women are about keeping a house a certain way. You can help keep a whole lot of peace around here by doing the little things." She also suggests that he could show that he cares by even making up the bed since he leaves for work after her.

"Oh, yes. I really do. I'm glad that we had this conversation."

Inwardly, he smirks at the thought that he bought himself time by appeasing her during that conversation. Besides, he reasons, what's the big deal about leaving a towel on the door? It wasn't an issue when she used to visit his place while they were dating just five years ago.

So the next day he leaves the towel on the door and never bothers to straighten up the bed. She returns home from work. It was a horrible day. And the first thing she notices is the bed, triggering an angry reaction. About two hours later he returns home from work; it's only when he places the key into the keyhole that he recalls what he didn't do that morning.

"Too late now; I guess I better face the fire," he says to himself. He might have had a chance at redeeming himself by bringing home a peace offering of some sort—a card, flowers, or both—but he didn't even do that.

"Didn't we talk about this yesterday?" she queries him. "You said that you would help out by putting away the towel. You just never listen, do you?"

He shrugs it off, walking towards the kitchen.

"I forgot. I got caught up into doing a few things before leaving for work; it slipped my mind."

"I know you didn't say that," she huffed. "It doesn't slip your mind to be patting me on my behind or shoulder about eleven o'clock at night—"

"Ah, that's something different."

"No it isn't. You never do anything around here. I'm not your maid. When I mentioned about us paying someone to straighten up the house, you say that we can't afford it. Oh, but you can afford to get off into that porn and gamble online. Something isn't right."

Let's presume at this point in their relationship it is a big thing for his wife that he recognizes the importance of keeping a clean place, although some wives learn over time not to major on the minor issues.

Rather than taking his wife's feelings into consideration, a selfish husband will think only of himself. Nothing else matters. Therefore, he will tune out on anything that his wife attempts to communicate with him.

Selfishness is nothing more than a byproduct of pride. When a person is full of pride, he or she views the world from only one perspective. That individual is blind to everything else in his or her environment; and in the communication process, dare it be said "listening impaired?"

Solomon wrote in Proverbs that "pride goes before destruction." The apostle Paul inferred that when an individual is full of pride that person lives in delusion because he (or she) makes the mistake of believing that he (or she) is something when they're not; therefore, that person deceives himself. (Galatians 6:3)

The reality is that nobody can force or manipulate an individual to listen to anybody. My wife often speaks of a person is faced with consequences for the decisions that are made, including ones that involve refusing to listening to wisdom or godly advice. Again, for the prideful husband he faces the possibility of his prayers being hindered; there's the potential that nothing that he aspires in life will ever come to fruition.

The husband who shows a sincere willingness to listen to his wife actually exudes an appealing quality of leadership: humility. The Bible declares that we are to serve one another. Jesus, whom Paul described as having humbled Himself to the point of death and the cross, posed the question to His disciples about who is really the greatest? It is the one who serves.

So what is the reward of humility? The Bible says God will exalt that person. (James 4:10)

And what is one of the rewards of a husband who listens to his wife? It is my experience that he automatically earns her respect.

Marriage and relationships commentator Jimmy Evans said the man who receives input from his wife sends the message that he values her ideas and feelings. "[A man's] need for esteem is important. But your wife's need to feel valued in the relationship is of equal importance."

'A man's need for esteem is important. But your wife's need to feel valued in the relationship is of equal importance'—Jimmy Evans

---

Evans and his wife, Karen, have been married for more than thirty-five years. In his many speaking engagements, he's shared with his audience how he maintained a chauvinistic and immature approach to his marriage. Additionally, he said his lack of understanding of a woman's nature being different from a man's was the reason why he often dismissed anything his wife might communicate with him.

As he underwent a change, Evans recognized when a husband values his wife's input it also makes her feel special and secure within a marriage. He added, "Few things hurt a woman more than to be rejected and devalued by her husband as she tries to share her viewpoints."

Psychological Noise

The examples of noise that are produced from within the husband's soul—pride and selfishness—might be a first cousin to what experts consider as **psychological** noise. This kind of noise is the preconceived notions, stereotypes, and assumptions that are brought into a conversation. It could also be a husband's bad attitude that could prevent any message from being decoded and effectively understood. Nothing the wife says matters to him.

Another common complaint I've identified in many marital situations is when the wife says the husband doesn't allow her to say anything without it becoming an argument. A nice way of describing a husband who hinders and distorts any message being transmitted is someone who lacks understanding. But a more direct way of describing a husband like that is foolish.

A foolish husband is not good for the marriage; his actions affect him, his wife, and the rest of the family. I'm reminded of the story of Nabal from the Bible. It described that he was very rich, owning thousands of heads of livestock. He was also a stubborn, cruel, insensitive, and evil man. It could also be said that God gave Nabal a wife, Abigail, who complemented him because she was a "woman of good understanding," or in today's terms very wise, and she had a disposition that was the opposite of him.

According to what transpired in 1 Samuel 25, David's servants approached Nabal about giving them food, clothing, and water. But Nabal refused to accommodate David. In fact, he commented, "Who is David, and who is the son of Jesse? There are many servants nowadays who break away each one from his master." (Verse 10)

Nabal's insult reminded me of something that occurred during the 1994 NFL draft. Former Indianapolis general manager Bill Tobin reacted to ESPN draft analyst Mel Kiper's criticism of the Colts' first-round draft pick with his famous "Who the hell is Mel Kiper, anyway?" remark.

Kiper appeared not to have taken Tobin's response personally, and he even commented that he was very much comfortable with his own analysis. Conversely, David took Nabal's remark very personal and resolved to wipe out Nabal and his entire household.

One of Nabal's servants reported to Abigail what transpired. He informed Abigail that David treated him and the rest of Nabal's servants well, and nothing was lost or harmed while David was with them. The servant, who warned Abigail of David's intent, even went as far as to describe Nabal as someone who listens to nobody.

Let's presume that Abigail knew that she could not convince her husband into apologizing to David and making peace with the king-in-waiting. That's probably why she took it upon herself to intercede on Nabal's behalf. "Please, let not my lord regard this scoundrel Nabal. For as his name is, so is he: Nabal [Fool] is his name, and folly is with him!

"And it shall come to pass, when the Lord has done for my lord according to all the good that He has spoken concerning you, and has appointed you ruler over Israel, that this will be no grief to you, nor offense of heart to my lord, either that you have shed blood without case, or that my lord has avenged himself. But when the Lord has dealt with my lord, then you remember your maidservant." (Verse 25, 30-31)

David acknowledged and heeded Abigail's advice that his conscience might be clear of bloodshed. He also accepted her peace offering and went his separate way. When Abigail returned, she found Nabal having a feast and he was very drunk. She did not apprise him of anything until the next morning; and when she did, he suffered a stroke upon hearing her words. He died ten days later.

God is so merciful to the husband who refuses to listen to his wife, but for how long? "[He] resists the proud but gives grace to the humble." (James 4:6)

External Noise

As a teenager, I remembered how much I loved playing loud music especially from groups like Led Zeppelin, Def Leppard, Creedence Clearwater Revival, and Black Sabbath. I didn't care that people in the neighborhood behind me were likely to hear it so long as it was being played. A strange thing occurred, however, as I've gotten older and became a parent. I'm often telling my daughter to turn down her music because it's a distraction especially when I'm working on something.

"That isn't music that you're playing, anyway, daughter."

"Oh, daddy, you don't know good music if it were staring you in the face!"

"No, *you* don't know good music. I've got plenty of it. I just don't blast it all over the house."

The most common noise that is associated with husbands not listening to their wives is the kind that is affected by sights, sounds, talking, smell, texture, and environment because it is **external** to the receiver. This was the part of Lomas' lecture on the Shannon-Webster model that I remember the most: He illustrated it by distancing himself from the classroom and yelling back to us as he articulated each example.

"Or you have factors like NOISE that can distort a message!" Lomas said much to the amusement of my classmates and me; I will also venture to say proximity may also affect the quality of the message that is received and decoded.

External noise is the most common associated with husbands not listening to their wives.

In the many online articles that I researched, the consensus was that removing the external noise was the most common solution women identified to get men to listen to them. As one suggested, "Turning off the TV might help. Guys are like kids; they are easily distracted by shiny, loud objects."

Some men may take offense to this because they feel that there is nothing wrong with them relaxing by watching a sporting event or some action movie. If it isn't a sporting event, they might not find anything wrong with unwinding by browsing the Internet, or perhaps playing an online game or two. So what annoys them is when a wife pops into their setting and asks for their attention. And when he does not immediately respond to her being there, she lets him know in no uncertain terms that she did not appreciate it.

"Hmmm, scream really loudly? No, that's not it," one woman pondered. "Stand naked before him? No, definitely not.

"I would say that making sure that there are no distractions (as in TV or radio playing the game) is important, and that you don't ambush him."

I'm not guilty of being engrossed into a sporting event on TV because for more than a decade I was paid to see them while I was a sports reporter. I can say without any shame that I've not seen an entire sporting event on television since I left the newspaper business. (I'm likely to fall asleep while watching one.) What I am guilty of is being engrossed in front of a computer screen or having a pair of headphones stuck in my ears listening to my many mp3 files.

Most times my wife has been very considerate of me, but I've also recognized that there have been plenty of times that I've disappointed her.

If a husband expects to have a happy marriage, he must learn to sacrifice the game, some time away from the computer, or any activity that hinders his attention while his wife is talking to him. After all, she is entitled to that measure of respect and consideration.

Okay, so you have his attention. Now what is it you want to share with him? All of a sudden, the husband begins to twist and turn his body. Maybe he does something like me where I find a spot on the floor to stretch—literally. Or maybe he's sprawled out wherever he is and he has his hands clasped behind his head and his eyes are closed.

"Well, honey, I've been thinking all day about something...," she says. "What is wrong with you? Can't you tell that I'm trying to talk to you?"

"Yeah, but I'm just trying to relax so that I can concentrate on what you're telling me."

"I don't understand. Why can't you do that before I talk to you? It looks like you really don't want to listen to anything I say."

"That's not true. I do want to listen. I was trying to get comfortable."

"Humph, well you need to get comfortable another time and another place, and not around me. Especially when I'm trying to talk to you!"

"Look, you complain about me not listening to you. When I am trying to listen to you, it's like you don't appreciate it. What is it you want? I'm not like your female friends. And I wish you wouldn't expect that from me."

"No, what I expect is that you just listen to me for a change."

The scenario just given may not be noise that distorts the woman's message being decoded and understood the by the man, but it is a distraction to the woman who wants so badly for him to listen to her. At some point they will need to find some common ground for conversation; otherwise, they are heading down a path that will lead to detachment or even worse—divorce.

Georgetown linguistics professor Deborah Tannen argues any impression of not listening might be the result of "misalignments in the mechanics of conversation" and this begins once the man and woman take their physical positions for the conversation.

According to her research, she recognized that girls start at an early age facing each other while they talk, and then maintaining eye contact. The boys, however, sat at an angle while they talked, gazed elsewhere, and periodically made eye contact. Answers and solutions to these misalignments were not psychological, where there is often someone to blame in the diagnosis, but were a part of a sociolinguistic approach that she saw as cross-cultural communication.

In other words, the man and woman should try to gain an understanding about each other's communicative behavior. So often we realize that nobody ever took the time out to explain why men and women are so different, let alone taking the time out ourselves to study the differences in the way we communicate.

"Once the problem is understood, improvement comes naturally," Tannen wrote in a *Washington Post* article; she notes it also diffuses the argument whether one person was right or wrong.

It is virtually impossible to set ourselves free from psychological noise; however, we must strive to recognize that it exists and we consider those distractions whenever we're faced with a similar scenario. In other words, we must be acutely aware of what we're doing. Some might call this being disciplined. Others might call it being wise.

Internal Noise

A husband's health (sickness or auditory), him daydreaming; or him being preoccupied, tired, hungry, or stressed out can also interfere or distort the message being transmitted to him. This type of noise is known as **internal** because it affects the individual internally.

A husband's health, him daydreaming; or him being preoccupied, tired, hungry, or stressed out can also interfere or distort the message being transmitted to him.

Some wives understand this and they try not to overwhelm their husbands.

"Well, he listens BUT he forgets a lot. I feel like we have the same conversations because he doesn't remember things," says one respondent within my social network. "I'll go ahead and make his excuse...he works a lot and he's always tired so his mind is bad."

In the times that we're living in, I'm going to make a reasonably safe statement that stress could be one of the single leading factors of noise for men. There's so much to consider. Job security is so unstable that nobody knows if there will be a job to go to the next day. More people are in debt and there seems to be fewer options to get out of it. Anxiety is the leading mental health problem in the United States. According to a 2000 National Institute of Mental Health study, more than 19 million Americans between the ages of eighteen and fifty-four suffer from some form of anxiety disorder.

Ronald Kessler, a professor of health care policy at Harvard School of Medicine, co-authored a study by the World Health Organization that mentioned the likelihood of developing an anxiety disorder had more than doubled since the 1970s.

According to a 2000 National Institute of Mental Health study, more than 19 million Americans between the ages of eighteen and fifty-four suffer from some form of anxiety disorder.

"It's a scary place and time. People are moving to strange cities, taking jobs in new industries; there's a lot of uncertainty about the future. Bad things that happen to people are on the rise," Kessler said in an October 2000 *USA Today Weekend* article. "Look at the evening news: murders, car accidents, terrorist bombs. This stuff is out there in the popular imagination and making us worried."

Under normal circumstances, women tend to become overwhelmed by life's stresses because they're constantly thinking about them. When women say they have a lot on their mind, they actually do. Where as, men typically handle stressful situations by simply focusing in on one particular thing; they are likely to compartmentalize emotions, information, and perceptions. Thus, that may explain why some women are taken aback when they recognize men seem so unemotional and detached during various crises.

That was essentially the way I handled matters when my marriage sunk to its lowest point a few years back. Rightly or wrongly, instead of catering to my marriage I decided to write books.

So can you imagine a woman who approaches her husband when he's preoccupied by a stressful situation?

Let's presume the wife is in another room in the house watching the television. The husband, who had a difficult day at work, went straight to the computer, browsing the ESPN.com website. This is his way of unwinding.

"Honey, I saw something on television that I wanted to talk to you about. You see, there was this lady on there talking about her marriage, and...aren't you listening to me?"

"Huh?"

"I said that I saw a lady on television talking about her marriage. She's dealing with some of the same things as we are."

Slow to glance up at her, he replies, "Really?" Then he resumes browsing the latest sports news.

Now the wife has few options. She can leave him alone, electing to revisit this topic at a later moment, which some recommend she should do. She could have a conniption and let him know, in no uncertain terms, that she did not appreciate him responding to her so blankly. Or she could try probing him in a loving, caring manner. There's always the possibility that he might open up to her and reveal to her that he's been under a lot of duress by life's circumstances. The challenge, though, is him being receptive to her.

"Women are a gift from God. Society is greatly benefited by the influence women bring to men. Without them, men are much less productive and much more dangerous to themselves and others... Let your wife know that you are thankful for her as you honor her ideas and feelings," writes Evans.

Perhaps the hardest thing men fail to recognize is that both spouses should be there for each other and not when it is convenient. This might explain why some wives feel that men listen to them only when they want to, or when it is in the man's best interests.

'A Matter of Semantics?'

I've reached a point in this chapter where I feel like I'm entitled to have a little fun. For the husband, this might be his only chance at creating an intelligible defense as to why he doesn't listen to his wife. It is known as **semantic** noise because there are times when a wife might pronounce words incorrectly or compose phrases (syntactically) that may not make any sense; therefore, it hinders his ability to listen to her.

Now if a man thinks he really has a chance to win the war of words with his wife, just remember this joke that I discovered online:

"Marriage is a relationship in which one person is always right and the other is a husband."

If understanding is the goal of all communication, semantics plays an important role. A husband may immediately tune out on his wife because he's already anticipated something unfavorable.

Here are some famous opening statements from a wife:

"When was the last time you (fill in the blank) . . ."

"Can you think of anything that we can do together?"

"Why don't you ever (fill in the blank) . . ."

"Honey, I've got something that I want to talk to you about..."

"Can you come here for a minute?"

And here is a husband's famous response to all of these inquiries: None.

We've all experienced having said something that was meant one way, but it was interpreted differently. I will be the first to say in my marriage that I've found myself on this side of the ledger on numerous occasions. Thus, I found another joke online that's given me some solace:

"My wife and I always compromise; I admit I'm wrong and she agrees with me."

If understanding is the goal of all communication, semantics plays an important role.

The wife is generally thought to be the more caring person compared to her husband because it is her nature to be nurturing of relationships. Therefore, she is likely to be more mindful of what she says to her husband because she does not want to offend him, anyway.

Ah, but nobody's perfect.

Let's presume that a husband and wife have been married for just a few months. It is her first marriage and his second. He's managed to overcome many of the emotional scars that he sustained from his first marriage. His ex-wife berated him at every opportunity. He discovered that she was unaccountable for much of the money spent. He suspected her of infidelity but he could never substantiate it. He filed for divorce citing irreconcilable differences.

Having gone on, he's learned how to love once again, or at the very least allow himself to be in love. He and his new wife just recently had a sexual encounter and afterward he shared a joke with her that he'd read from the Internet.

Smiling in his embrace, she says, "Oh, baby, you can be so stupid."

For a moment, his body tenses; he has no feeling.

"What's wrong?" she inquires.

He sits up in bed, staring straight ahead. "Uh, why did you say that?" He sighs.

"Is there something wrong with what I said? We just made wild, passionate love and I'm in a good mood. Aren't you?"

He shakes his head. At least to him her response is beyond distorted. His mind is now racing a thousand miles per minute.

"I knew we shouldn't have done this," he grimaces.

"Done what?"

"Look, if you think that you can just marry me and talk to me just any way, you're going to be very disappointed."

"What are you talking about?"

"No, what are *you* talking about!"

"You're being selfish," she argues. "I think you need to get out of here . . . Now!"

He counters, "Maybe you should get out of here. Yeah, I might have married you for love, but I sure is hell didn't marry you to talk to me just any kind of way. I'm not letting it happen.

"No sir!"

Then he quickly gets dressed and storms out of their apartment to cool off. Several hours passed before they attempt to reconcile their differences. The husband calls before he returns home and apologizes to his wife for reacting to her the way he did. He explains to her that he didn't realize that he still struggled with some of the emotional scar from his first marriage.

"If I knew that, I would have never said the word 'stupid.' I thought you understood what I meant," she says. "I know you're not that way. You're one of the most intelligent, thoughtful men I've ever known. That's why I accepted your marriage proposal."

"I didn't know that I would react so angrily to a word like stupid, as well. Now I understand why some people have flashbacks to a traumatic event in their lives. It just happened to me."

"The last thing I want to do is upset you over something I've said. I'm sorry."

"I'm sorry, too."

Semantic noise is not limited to verbal messages. It includes the non-verbal realm of communication. So that means a wife's body language, behavior, and gestures might also distort a message, or at the very least is not fully understood or accurately decoded by the husband.

Semantic noise is not limited to verbal messages. It includes the non-verbal realm of communication.

Here's a classic one: It's early in the morning. A husband and wife are lying in bed together. She reaches over and strokes his body. He reacts to her touch thinking that she's interested in accommodating him for sex, but all she meant was showing a moment of affection while she was nuzzled up to him.

"All you do is think about sex," she reacts, turning over in bed. "What's wrong with us just cuddling up to each other?"

"Hey, don't touch me unless you want to do something. That's all I have to say about it."

"Humph. Why don't you bother to figure out that men and women think differently about sex? And don't think that I'm in any mood right now!"

When it is a matter of semantics, the husband could have helped himself out greatly if he'd taken a moment to think about his wife's message and then ask her what she really meant. In a calm and non-agitated manner, he could have also repeated or paraphrased what she just said for better understanding.

Most research indicate that men are not good at asking for help when they are lost—even when they are having difficulty navigating their way through a troubled relationship—or admitting when they're wrong. Thus, bad habits take time to overcome. So often, however, men are quick to react to these misunderstandings either rightly or wrongly justified.

A wife could also help herself out by thinking through exactly what she wants to communicate with him because not everything she says is clear—or dare I even say correct. There are things she might say that are easily understood among women, but not necessarily among men. So she must make sure that whatever she has to say to him is in terms that he can understand.

IN REVIEW:

- Noise is anything that can distort or interfere with understanding and decoding a message in the communication process.
- There are four general categories of noise in communication: external, semantic, psychological, and internal.
- A husband can help himself gain greater understanding of his wife's message by simply asking questions.
- A wife can improve a husband's ability to understand what she says by transmitting messages (verbal or nonverbal) in terms that he can understand.

Completing the Communication Process: Feedback

According to the Shannon-Weaver model, **feedback** is what completes the communication process as the receiver transmits his or her thoughts, opinion, or information back to the sender. It also provides the sender a gauge as to whether there was any understanding of his or her message.

In a marital model, it is my opinion that spouses not only seek meaningful feedback from each other, but it defines whether either spouse has acted upon or not acted upon the other spouse's message. Husbands tend to be guilty of not providing feedback in the form of words spoken and/or by his non-verbal communication or behavior.

"It's very important," says one female social network respondent. "It shows that [he] cares enough to really listen and participate, and not pacify."

For example, the last thing a wife wants to experience after she's lectured or preached to her husband for twenty minutes on the virtues and benefits about taking her out is a response that has no relation to the topic.

"Yeah, uh, that sounds like a good idea," he answers. "But did you know that I really need to change the oil before we do that?"

"Did you not hear anything that I've said?"

"Of course I did. You said we need to go out every now and then."

"Yes, and?"

There is silence.

"I said the reason why you need to take me out is because it shows that you really want to invest into our marriage. Now do you understand what I'm talking about?"

"Honestly, I think you're just nagging at me," he answers. "You need to stop looking at all of those Lifetime Channel movies. I think they're giving you bad ideas."

"Is that all you have to say?" the wife retorts. "One of these days you're going to realize what you've had. I hope it isn't too late—"

Spouses not only seek meaningful feedback from each other but it defines whether either spouse has acted upon or not acted upon the other spouse's message.

A leading reason why some women become involved in extramarital affairs is because another man gives her the attention—and feedback—that she's lacking at home.

"I find it very attractive when your partner can carry a meaningful conversation," admitted one female respondent; she did not indicate whether she was single or married. "I also find it quite stimulating."

When women communicate among themselves, feedback is very much a part of their expressive nature. "It would be very disrespectful to me if he didn't have anything to say," says another female social network respondent. "It doesn't have to be meaningful, but I demand some feedback to let me know I'm not talking to myself."

Just the very thought of a man's unwillingness or inability to afford his wife the courtesy of being an active participant in his marriage in areas that do not involve sex evokes comparisons of raising children. There was once a time I would be offended whenever I'd hear a woman make reference to her man either jokingly or derisively as a child, but not any more. It does seem to be a sophomoric thing if a grown man has to be constantly reminded and badgered by his wife into doing the basics things of a marriage: love, honor, and respect.

The Bible exhorts us to mature in all areas of our life. So it should be understood a wife is not a husband's mother; the man should only cleave to her, forming a bond and relationship that cannot be easily broken. But many men enter into marriages having no examples of how to conduct themselves as men and husbands. These same men do not help themselves at all when they allow their ego or outside sources of opinions that are aimed at destroying what they have hinder them from even seeking the necessary knowledge and wisdom.

"But solid food belongs to those who are of full age, that is, those who by reason of use have their senses exercised to discern both good and evil.

"Therefore, leaving the discussion of elementary principles of Christ, let us go on to perfection, not laying again the foundation of repentance from dead works and of faith toward God . . ." (Hebrews 5:14, 6:1)

Much of what has been discussed in this book are reasonably simple things to follow. But with many of life's pursuits, it is the elementary things that must be applied if an individual has any expectation of moving forward. Admittedly, some of the ideas and topics I've shared are the very things that I once ignored my wife, mocked individuals who tried imparting wisdom to me, or I simply chose not to apply in my life.

How can a man, therefore, expect his woman to respect him when he's done nothing in his marriage that makes him deserving of her respect? The husband who fails to recognize this deceives himself, and he's nothing more than a hypocrite.

When a husband provides his wife meaningful feedback as reflective of the things he does and say, it becomes a testament of just how serious he takes his marriage and how much he regards his wife as an equal partner in it. Also, the way a Christian man manages his relationship with his wife is also a reflection of his relationship with God: He should always be striving toward the prize of the higher calling that is within him. And just as he strives toward maturity, he makes himself an example for his wife to follow in the same. Only God can inspire this is a form of love.

"So husbands ought to love their own wives as their own bodies; he who loves his wife loves himself." (Ephesians 5:28)

When a husband provides his wife meaningful feedback as reflective of the things he does and say, it becomes a testament of just how serious he takes his marriage and how much he regards his wife as an equal partner in it.

My wife, who is by far the more observant one between us, often has shared with me the state of a man's marriage is made transparent through his wife's non-verbal behavior whenever they're in public.

"I don't want to be like some of the women I see while we're driving on the freeway who are looking away from the man who's driving," she says. "That's a dead giveaway that she wants nothing to do with him and he has no clue. He's just talking away while they're driving and she isn't saying anything other than 'I don't want to look at him [and] I really don't want to say anything to him.'"

Although many husbands may not have received any formal instruction on how they should listen to their wives, some have been given hints through their professional training how to effectively listen to and provide appropriate feedback to their wives.

Some of the hints that I'd been equipped with came from my career in print journalism, but for many years I never utilized them. Half of the ten attributes that Giles taught me toward being a good journalist also had application to becoming a better husband: a keen observer, empathy, sensitivity, openness, and a good listener.

As it was explained to me in that Journalism 101 class, a keen observer will have a much wider perspective about his interview opportunity. Rather than being solely intent on just asking questions, a good journalist will be observant of the environment and the other person's verbal and non-verbal communication.

Women tend to recognize the different inflections of words spoken and various ways that the other person reacts to questions asked, or even the depth and extent of a person's silence. They are observant of the other person's clothing, posture, and gestures.

If a husband takes the time to observe his wife, he might learn a thing or two about her that he may not have known. That could be the difference in him becoming a better husband. The way an individual processes these observations will also affect the quality of his or her feedback.

A keen observer, empathy, sensitivity, and openness are traits of a husband becoming a good listener.

When women communicate, they tend to seek agreement and an emotional connection, which leads to them bonding and establishing more friendships. And by their expressive and emotional nature women are better adept at understanding the other person's thoughts, emotions, and feelings. This is empathy. Another word for it is compassion.

Jesus is the Christian husband's example of someone who has empathy toward others. The Bible also describes how we have a savior who understands the many temptations and weaknesses that we have because He was in all points tempted. (Hebrews 4:15) For that reason, Jesus is our advocate before the Father. (1 John 1:8) He is the reason why we can run boldly to the throne of grace in a time of need (Hebrews 4:16)—I'm willing to express in this book that Jesus is a husband's biggest cheerleader for getting things right with his wife.

An empathetic husband does not make snap judgments repeatedly. When his wife speaks, he is not quick to tune out on her simply because he doesn't like hearing her voice, or anything she has to say. He understands that it is very disrespectful to cut somebody off without hearing the conclusion of the whole matter. He also understands the manner in which he values her input and contributions has an effect on the way she opens up to him emotionally—and even sexually—in his marriage.

A husband should be encouraged to respond appropriately, meaning that he needs to take into consideration what he says and how he reacts to his wife according to his non-verbal communication and behavior. This is sensitivity.

Let's use an example of a husband who is not sensitive to his wife's mentioning that she is allergic to chocolate. (For some individuals, chocolate is actually an aphrodisiac because there is a chemical within it that causes individuals to become more in tuned with their feelings of love.[4]) The couple had been married at the time for two years. The husband decided to surprise his wife with flowers and chocolate candy; he experienced both the thrill of victory and agony defeat in one effort.

The wife reacts, "Why did you buy me chocolate? Haven't I told you that I'm allergic to it?"

"I guess you did tell me," the husband answers. "I forgot."

"You what? Did you say that you forgot?" she screams. "You know what, you've never listened to anything that I've ever told you. What you just did tells me that you've never really cared about me at all. We've been together for two years, and this is all that you can do for me?"

Now the husband is equally indignant because his wife did not appreciate his effort. "Humph. I call myself getting you something for your birthday. Next time, do it yourself!"

There's a good chance that this husband's birthday gift will forever live in infamy with his wife. This could have been avoided had he listened to her and been sensitive to her having allergic reactions to chocolate. Another lesson in that exchange is that he should have been candid in his feedback, yet respectful.

The manner in which [a husband] values [his wife's] input and contribution[s] has an effect on the way she opens up to him emotionally—and even sexually—in his marriage.

If there's been anything that has marked my relationship with my wife it would be our candor toward each other, although there have been more than a few times the candor has had an edge to it that cut rather deep and drawn a lot of blood. This is why the Bible exhorts husbands and wives to be kind to one another, tenderhearted and forgiving, even as Christ forgave us (Ephesians 4:32), because it is human nature to defend ourselves from hurtful comments and then retaliate with words and actions that we deem as appropriate to the injury that we've sustained.

A husband who is not closed minded to every thought, opinion, or suggestion by his wife is one who possesses traits of openness.

According to Matthew 27:19, Roman governor Pontus Pilate failed to heed his wife, Claudia Procula, about the charges that were conspired against Jesus. She had a dream that Jesus was innocent and she implored her husband not give into the Jews' request that He be crucified. "Have nothing to do with that just Man, for I have suffered many things today in a dream because of him," she said.

Some argue that Pilate's name would not be as vilified as Judas' throughout time had he resisted his pride, the intense lobbying by the chief priests and elders, and the crowd that demanded for Jesus. Of all the possibilities, God could have very well given Pilate multiple signs not to be the person who handed Jesus over to be crucified. But the Bible notes that God used only Claudia Procula to tell Pilate otherwise.

It is noted that Pilate symbolically cleared himself of his offense by washing his hands before the crowd. "I am innocent of the blood of this just Person. You see to it." (Matthew 27:24) And while Jesus' death by crucifixion was the fulfillment of scripture, can one imagine the conversation that Pilate had with Jesus when he stood before the Judgment Seat?

Neither spouse knows everything. And neither spouse is so correct in his or her way of doing things that theirs is the standard by which all things are done. Sometimes they just have different approaches to accomplishing the same task.

This was another realization Marilyn McCoo admitted about her perfectionist streak when dealing with her husband, Billy Davis., Jr.

"Instead of arguing about the fastest way to LAX, I let Billy drive the route he wanted to go," she said. "Funny, but we always made good time to the airport—and we both arrived less stressed."

Personally, I've read the parable of the talents (Matthew 25 14-30) many times, and I've made application of it in various conversations and essays. One thing that's consistent in my commentaries of it is management skills. Although the husband is seen by God as the head of the household, he has been given help to make more effective decisions; a good manager utilizes all of his resources that are available to him.

The worst thing he can do is nothing. That is the husband who runs off and hides and he avoids responsibility in his marriage. Therefore, I'm convinced that a husband, despite some inherent weaknesses, is given grace and the ability of reasoning to seek help when he's lacking in various areas in his life.

Some of the changes that have occurred in my life have been the result of me doing just that. And once I've reached an understanding with it, I also realize that I'll be judged by it.

So now the question is what is a good listener? By now if a husband applies any of the information I've shared thus far in a useful way, he will be on the road to becoming a good listener. That husband will know in the way his wife responds and reacts to him.

IN REVIEW:

- Feedback is what completes the communication process as the receiver transmits his or her thoughts, opinion, or information back to the sender.
- Feedback also provides the sender a gauge as to whether there was any understanding of his or her message.
- The manner in which a husband values his wife's input and contribution[s] has an effect on the way she opens up to him emotionally—and even sexually—in his marriage.
- A keen observer, empathy, sensitivity, and openness are traits that will help a husband become a good listener. And meaningful feedback enhances a marriage relationship.

Why He Doesn't Listen: A Husband's Scientific Excuse?

I've been known by some as being a resourceful, self-reliant, and somewhat industrious individual. Translated, I've had a knack for figuring out a thing or two under the hood of a car and then making the necessary repairs. Sometimes I can engage in a highly fluent conversation with a paid automotive professional. My challenge has been articulating to my wife the intricate details of making the repairs. But she's like most women: her only concern is whether her car has gas in it, it starts, and it can safely get her from Point A to Point B.

Thus, she could care less, for example, if her power steering pump requires a fourteen millimeter socket for the power steering belt's tension bearing, the bracket for the high pressure line, or the bolts that holds the power steering pump onto its bracket; or for that matter, a nineteen millimeter socket for the power steering belt pulley and high pressure connection.

"Well, that's nice," is about all she'd say. "Now, are you sure that nothing else wrong with this car?"

"Uh, I think so," is about as best of an answer I might give her. "You may not want to hear this, but the only other thing that might go wrong is with the rack and pinion, a part that costs about $600 . . ."

"I'm going to pray that it isn't," she might say. "Now can I use the keys to your car?"

Guys love to show that they are capable of being productive, and in my opinion it is seemingly incumbent upon them to be just that. Therefore, I've probably expected for my wife to show some interest in what I've had to say since it was *her car* that was being worked on. Especially since I figured that I had explained things in such a way that even she could understand such nuances.

Now invariably at some point in the day my wife has had similar expectations of interacting with me. As much as I'd like to think that I'm different than most men, I suppose there are aspects about me that suggests that I'm not. I might be able to hang in there with my wife if she were to initiate a conversation with me about cooking since I do cook. I'm inclined to say that we'd be able to exchange opinions and information about the use of spices, and how long something needs to be marinated, cooked, boiled, or baked.

Some how, I've been guilty of showing a disconnection when the conversation shifts to something of this tenor:

"Let's talk about us," she'd say.

"What is it you want to talk about?"

"Well, it's like this. We need to work more on being as one with each other. We need to spend time getting into the word and praying. Sometimes, I don't feel like you really understand why I can be upset with you –"

On more than an occasion or two, I've started squirming wherever I've been sitting. Maybe I've begun to roll my eyes or take a deep breath. "What is it I'm doing wrong now?"

"I've been telling you all along that it takes more than what you're doing. Sure, you fix the car and you take care of things around the house; I appreciate that. But it's the little things that really make a difference."

By now, I've begun what I'll describe as a mental deceleration. Ever so smoothly, I'm not processing her words. Ever so obviously, she's not pleased with my reaction. Thus she'll inquire, "You are listening to me, aren't you?"

"Yeah, I'm listening to you. What do you want me to do? Tell you exactly what you just said?"

"Don't get smart with me."

"I'm not. You think that I'm ignoring you, and that's not fair." Now I've gotten up and I've headed to a neutral corner, so to speak. "Hey, didn't we talk about *us* just last night?"

"You still don't get it, do you?"

"Get what? That it seems I never do anything good enough for you?"

Sighing, my wife has now gone to her neutral corner, and that usually means the next round is likely to be contested when I least expect it. For the longest, I had failed to realize that unresolved issues with my wife only leads to unwanted and unnecessary stress and tension that could have been resolved had I been more engaged in the conversation with her—and had begun to do the little things that she had pointed out to me on numerous occasions.

Does any of this sound familiar? I'm going to make a safe and calculated bet that it does.

I'm sure women have wondered why men have such a limited capacity when it comes to listening just as much as men have wondered why women can initiate conversations that are of no interest and priority to them.

Now the godly explanation is that God created man and woman. Our differences, as complex as they may be, also makes it one of the most inexplicable wonders why men and women attract to each other. In a marriage, the husband is charged with dwelling with his wife with understanding (1 Peter 3:7) while the wife is charged with submitting to and respecting her husband (Ephesians 5:22, 33). And some way, some how, we are to do these things as unto the Lord, which gives Him glory because a marriage relationship should be a reflection of Christ's relationship with the church.

The scientific explanation is that men and women are wired differently, and the proof within our brains. The average person can speak at a rate of between 100 and 175 words per minute and think at a rate of 600 to 800 words per minute. According to a study by the Indiana University School of Medicine (November 2000), it indicated that men actually listen to women but perhaps with half of their brain.

Twenty men and women were asked to wear specially designed headphones while listening to an audio cassette of John Grisham's movie *The Partner* as it was played forward and then backward. Their brain activity was monitored by functional magnetic resonance imaging (*f*MRI). These images measured the blood flow to various parts of the brain – specifically in the left temporal lobe where listening and speech activity is associated where as non-verbal communication is processed with the right side of the brain. The study revealed when playing the movie forward that men used only the left side of their brain when listening to language while women used both sides.

"Our research suggests language processing is different between men and women, but it doesn't necessarily mean performance is going to be different," said Dr. Joseph T. Lurito, an assistant professor of radiology at Indiana's School of Medicine.

"We don't know if the difference is because of the way we're raised, or if it's hard-wired in the brain."

Men actually listen to women but perhaps with half of their brain.

Other research has determined that the very hormones we produce—testosterone (men) and estrogen (women)—also have an effect in our brain development and neural connections. Because a male's brain is likely to have less capacity for word use and word production, according to the Indiana School of Medicine study, he's more than likely to tune out of a conversation quicker than a woman.

It is also known that men tend process information more analytically than women, who conversely are more intuitive. This is because men predominately use their left side of the brain while women tend to have a greater capacity of also using their right side of the brain.

The left side of the brain is where analysis occurs, as well as operations of logic, planning, and detail. It is attuned to time, judging speed, and it is known to process more complicated information such as higher math (calculus, linear algebra, probability and theory) or quantum physics. The brain's left side is also regarded as the non-emotional side, yet emotions of happiness and optimism are also known to be traced back to there.

Renowned psychiatrist and clinical neuroscientist Dr. Daniel Amen observed, "When the left hemisphere is hurt, people are often depressed, negative, and irritable...[and] a consistent brain-imaging finding in major depression is low activity in the left-front side of the brain."

So does this mean that men are a bunch of RoboCops and Dr. Spocks and they are void of emotion? I suppose that's open for debate. Especially if someone were to ask my wife about me, since she's often chided me for being insensitive and non-caring during the early days of our dating, and for that matter earlier years of our marriage.

For example, over the years she's had great fun about reminding me of my infamous tire comment that occurred outside of her apartment while we were dating. One afternoon I made the remark that one of the tires on my Mustang 5.0 cost more than all four tires on her Mazda 323. She felt that I had insulted her although I knew deep within that I had no malicious intentions.

I tried explaining to her that I had recently done some price shopping for tires and her car triggered a memory of that.

"So what does all that has to do with my car?" she snapped back at me. "And why was it necessary that you even had to mention it?"

I answered that I previously owned two cars with similar tire sizes, so I had some working knowledge as to how much it would cost to replace tires on her car. Needless to say, that didn't go over well, and all I did was pushed my size twelve's farther inside my mouth.

"First of all," she replied, "are you trying to insinuate that I need tires on my car?"

"Uh, no—"

"Then why did you bring it up in the first place?"

Years later, I mentioned the story to an older man. He chuckled at me. "You know you shouldn't have said that. I understand what you were trying to tell her, but with women it doesn't work."

I conceded, "Yeah, I know. She hasn't let that one die down, and that was over fifteen years ago."

My wife would make the argument that I lacked wisdom in that situation, and the Bible offers that if anyone lacks in it to ask God for it; He's more than willing to give it. That may be true. It is also likely if there had been more activity on my right side of the brain then I would have had a sense for recognizing that I'd said the wrong thing about those tires. Activity on the brain's right side is associated with knowing when problems arise, or when individuals are attuned to hunches; it is also the side where anxiety is processed.

Perhaps this, too, might explain why women are more emotional than men because their right side is more active. Hence, this is why some women may feel that men must do more to appeal to them, or why men complain that women demand much more from them when they feel that they've already done enough.

So many times my wife has said, "I'm a woman and you should know that we're more emotional. You can't just walk away from me whenever you don't agree with something I've told you. If you want to see better results in this marriage, you've got to figure out that I need much more than you're giving me."

In the early days of our marriage, I was inclined to respond, "Yeah, but didn't it count for anything that I did what you asked of me *yesterday?*"

"That was yesterday. Now what are you going to do about today?"

"Come on, are you going to remind me of every single thing that I'd done wrong or hadn't done at all?"

The average male brain capacity is larger than a female's having more cells and neurons, but a woman's production of estrogen facilitates more connections from one side of her brain to the other. Dr. Amen notes according to some studies that a woman's *corpous collosum*, a fiber that connects both sides, is larger than in men[5]. This may explain why women tend to use both sides of their brain while processing language; and for that reason, men may be more one-track minded and handle singular tasks where as women have a greater capacity to multi-task conversations and perform other operations and they never seem to be lost.

Women have a greater capacity to multi-task conversations and perform other operations and they never seem to be lost.

Interestingly, some of the listeners of my popular Internet-based talk show, *Maverick Media (on Blog Talk Radio),* have shared how they've found it impressive that I'm able to effectively host my show alone given that I'm performing several tasks: I'm usually working as many as three social networks giving people updates of the show's content or encouraging them to call in; I'm working the show's chat room and interacting with those listeners; I'm managing the show's switchboard for incoming phone calls or playing uploaded content as I've planned; and I'm also engaged in a conversation with my show's guests.

Perhaps it's because I view hosting my show as a singular task. But when I'm working on a book or editing a client's manuscript, I'm not one for playing music or maintaining phone conversations. It has to be quiet. I have to be focused solely on what I'm transferring from thought to computer, or I'm easily distracted.

While I'm at it, I'll share that if my wife asks me to go to the store for her, it's almost an automatic thing that I'll forget one item and it's usually the item that is most important to her. I've written lists, or my wife has given me a list, and I've still come up short. What has worked best for me is whenever she sends me a text message once she knows I'm in the store—yet there's always that distinct possibility of me forgetting something.

I suppose there are still not enough connectors making contact with the right side of my brain – and talking about dealing with the cards that I've been dealt!

Okay, so it's probably safe to agree that with greater brain activity, women are likely to be more expressive and have a tendency to have more to say during a conversation and that may explain why men complain that women talk...and talk...and talk...and talk.

This may also explain why men tune out, or transmit non-verbal messages that might suggest that they're not listening. And if there must be any further elaboration, it's probably because they can only handle so much or their brains might overload! But I'm inclined to believe women are intuitive to know this already.

Says one female social network respondent, "He tries but we as females tend to ramble on and on so they can only retain but so much...But I love the fact that he tries and he tends to retain the things that really matter."

Most women, therefore, understand the best way of helping a man to effectively listen to them is to get straight to the point. Give him the bottom line. Talk in terms that he can understand.

One woman suggested, "I find that I need to be direct with him...Put it on paper since men are visual. Give him facts, the price, and some time to think it over. "

Another theory is that people simply have a tendency to do the opposite of what's requested of them, or when their freedom or when their autonomy is being threatened. Psychologists refer to this as "reactance." This behavior is both conscious and subconscious.

People simply have a tendency to do the opposite of what's requested of them, when their freedom, or when their autonomy is being threatened.

In a study conducted by Tanya Chartrand, Amy Dalton, and Gavin Fitzsimmons, they present a case that reactance may be triggered subconsciously; the behavior is virtually automatic [6]. "Sometimes individuals feel compelled to behave in opposition to social influences." The social influence could be a boss, parent, friend, or spouse.

This determination was derived from two experiments. The first one studied twenty-four male and female psychology students from a university located in the Midwest. They were asked to list people who would most want them to achieve ten goals, including "work hard" and "have fun," and then rate the people according to each goal.

"These results suggest that for individuals who perceive a significant other to be highly controlling subliminally priming the name of that significant other causes these individuals to automatically do the opposite of that which the significant other wishes."

The goal of the second study was to confirm the results of the first. It theorized that people are more likely to react in opposition to the relationship partner whom they feel is controlling them because they inherently believe people are just out to control them.

This experiment studied 113 male and female students from a college in the Southeast. Among other things, they were also asked to list people who would most likely want them to achieve ten goals. The stated goal like "relax" replaced the goal of "having fun." And names that might trigger the responses were replaced with a string of letters. The results suggested the contrast between working hard and relaxing was a function of the level of reactance within an individual. (There was actually a higher level of resistance when people were asked to work harder than relax; however, it did not fully explain their hypothesis.)

What satisfied the experiment was the relationship of reactance to individuals who were perceived as controlling. "Significant others perceived as controlling can lead to automatic reactance in individuals; individuals chronically high in reactant tendencies, who see everyone as controlling, automatically react against significant others' wishes," the study concluded.

Studies also indicate women produce more of a bonding hormone known as oxytocin. This hormone, which is released through the pituitary gland, is more present in men after orgasm; it may also explain why men are likely to talk and be more connected after sex or feel sleepy after orgasm.

Oddly enough, women have more receptors for serotonin, the hormone that is associated with calming a person down in situations of anxiety and depression; it is commonly known as a "feel good" hormone and low levels of it has also been associated when people find themselves in love with someone. Mood swings in individuals are more likely to occur when there are lower levels of serotonin.

Now if my wife were to approach me about accompanying her to the mall on a shopping excursion she's already lost me. Chances are that if I know what's best for me, I'll accompany her. But my wife probably has a good idea that if she were to go into great detail about shopping for clothes, shoes, a purse, and make-up, the only response I'm likely to make is, "How much is all this going to cost?"

"Why are you always worried about how much something's going to cost?" she'd react. "Can't you just enjoy going out with your wife and us being together?"

Needless to say, I'll have a case of the creeps. And for somebody like me who's been very pro-male, I'm not sure if I'm so quick to own up to any scientific data that I've reacted to her with only half of my brain. But I may own up to my serotonin level decreasing sharply whenever she asks me to accompany her on a shopping spree.

As I pondered these scientific facts, the theological argument to a husband's inability to listen, or for that matter anyone's inability to listen, would be that we are sinful and rebellious by nature.

The apostle Paul wrestled with this truth in Romans 7 18-25:

"For I know that in me (that is, in my flesh) nothing good dwells; for to will is present with me, but how to perform what is good I do not find. For the good that I will to do, I do not do it; but the evil I will not to do, that I practice.

"Now if I do what I will not do, it is no longer I who do it, but sin that dwells in me. I find then a law, that evil is present with me, the one who wills to do good. For I delight in the law of God according to the inward man. But I see another law in my members, warring against the law of my mind, and bringing me into captivity the law of sin which is in my members.

"O wretched man that I am. Who will deliver me from this body of death? I thank God—through Jesus Christ our Lord! So then, with the mind I myself serve the law of God, but with the flesh the law of sin."

Lord, help us all!

More so, God knew exactly what He was doing when he created man and woman. Ideally, we are to complement each other and somehow help perfect each other so that we can truly reflect the fullness of Christ.

Another reality that continues to amaze me occurs whenever I stop and study my daughter, who is a product of both my wife and me. She possesses qualities and traits—both good and bad—that can be directly traced to her parents. It makes me acknowledge that God also knew what he was doing when he allowed me to meet who eventually became my wife, although there have been moments when I've been like Adam and lash out at Him by making the excuse "the woman that You gave me."

I muse that there are some things that just can't be solved through science. They require interpersonal contact. The Bible mentions that iron sharpens iron (Proverbs 27:17); or in more humanly terms, egos and personalities sharpens the individual. It is therefore unlikely that a husband can fully hide behind scientific data for his inability to listen to his wife and some how maintain a successful and satisfying marriage.

First of all, a wife is not going to allow it without bringing the deficiency – or deficiencies – to his attention. This is why a wife is perceived as nagging to her husband. Secondly, if he has any expectations that his wife will reciprocate respect or due affections to him, he will have to resolve any lingering issues with her. Unresolved issues lead to a wife shutting down on her husband emotionally and, yes, even sexually.

So what is a husband to do?

It's easy to say pray about it. It's also easy to say seek God through His word about it. But here are some things that I've done and also studied that has helped me to become an effective husband at listening to my wife:

- **Make a conscious decision that you're going to listen to your wife no matter how much it might annoy you.** The first and most important thing that a husband can do is have the resolve within to say that he will become a better man by making the effort that he's going to listen to his wife whenever she talks. He will recognize that she is a joint heir in the grace of God and she is a reflection of his success or failure; a wife should be an equal partner in a marriage relationship; and she should add to their union and not delete from it. There are times that husbands consciously tune out on wives because they simply don't want to hear what they have to say. That is disrespectful especially if she's been somebody who has had his best interest at heart. That is a tough thing to recognize when there is dissatisfaction brewing within a relationship. But with a sober mind, it is possible that a husband can identify qualities about his wife that validates her existence in his life.

- **Make your wife a priority in your life.** When a husband acknowledges that he needs improvement in this area, it is an indication that he's setting proper relational priorities. For the Christian man, the priorities should always be God, wife, family, and the rest. He should not always be reminded of this by his wife or for that matter a pastor or someone else with a perspective worth considering (hint, hint!). Wives respond to a husband who treats her as she's truly the queen in his life. They also respond to kindness and consideration, and a man who *listens* to her.

- **Realize that listening is not an easy thing to do.** Okay, so here's where a husband should acknowledge that his brain may not have the same capacity to process words like his wife. But with most skills it can be acquired with practice, patience, willingness, attentiveness, and consistency.

Listening with Sincerity

For any relationship that's worth having, one must put talk and thoughts into action. A spouse must make the other spouse the top priority in his or her life. If the spouse(s) is a professed Christian, the relationship with the other spouse should be akin to his or her relationship with their savior, and they must make a sincere effort at doing the things that each spouse would be most appreciative of.

My wife has often lectured to me that a woman appreciates the little things done for her. At times, my wife would ask me if I could relate to her any examples by what she meant. My immediate response was that I paid the bills, I worked, and I was capable of cooking, cleaning, sewing and ironing clothes for myself. She then asked me if I really knew how to be romantic; all I will say is that I made a move that she compared to the *RoboCop* movie character.

Disappointed, she graciously replied, "It's a lot more than that. I hope one day you'll get it." Then she began giving me examples of the "little things" that women appreciate, all of which went right over my head as though I were inside a wind tunnel. There was no drag in that marital coefficient because I had already tuned out on her.

Admittedly, I had no clue as to what the little things were because up to that point in life I had never been challenged in that area. So out of sarcasm and rebellion I thought the little things were just examples of a man being less than manly. They were ultimately nothing more than sure-fire ways of seeing one's self as hen pecked along with a few other less-than-reputable adjectives.

From time to time, my wife would also point out examples of men on television who at least appeared to have figured out what it took to build a successful marriage and family dynamic. I'm sure she thought that I would appreciate her thinking of me to point out what others had already done for their spouse. But I'd become so incensed with her and feeling brow-beaten into watching these men that I'd tell her that maybe she needed to find somebody just like them.

"It's not like that," she'd answer.

"So what!" I'd snarl back at her.

Depending on who might be reading this book (or is being implored to read it), I'm sure that there may be a similar reaction as to what I've shared so far. Eyes rolling. Huffing. Snorting. Cursing. Slinging the book to the side. I've done it as well in the past. And guess what? You're entitled to do that. Yet I'll challenge you this way: Is your marriage any better today than what it was yesterday or even last week?

It took me nearly five years into my marriage before I began fathoming what my wife had been trying to tell me, but I was inconsistent and lethargic at applying what I knew.

The little things are the things that a man does from the heart. If he gives her a card, it's because he wants to give her one. It's not out of compulsion after she's nagged and complained until he can no longer stand it. More importantly, he wants to see the smile on her face as a result of receiving it. That's an act of volition and out of sincerity.

The little things are also gestures and acts of kindness that do not need any reminders given by his wife: For example, bringing her something from the store that he knows she likes (i.e., flowers). In my household, my wife loves fruit, and during the summer months, she's a fanatic for watermelon, honeydew melons, or cantaloupe. And if I really want to score major points all I need to do is get her a whopper of a sweet watermelon without her asking me to get one, and maybe a "Thinking of You" card.

Other examples include me taking her out to lunch or dinner when it was not expected. Or there was the incident that occurred on a hot summer afternoon when my wife contacted me about her having a flat tire. Although I was headed to an appointment dressed in a white shirt, tie and wearing slacks, I turned around and drove to the location where her car was parked. I removed the tire, took it to a shop and had it replaced, and about a half-hour later put the new tire on her car.

Now women are very perceptive by nature. They're often good at discerning our thoughts and intents. Some call it intuition.

Translated, it means that if a husband wants to bring out the best in his wife, he needs to do the good and righteous things that pertain to his marriage. I'll even venture to say doing it with a sense of sincerity and integrity because nobody appreciates being played by another person who had ulterior motives. And if a wife's been used by a husband – if that wife's like mine – it will be an issue that does not easily die down. More than likely, he'll be reminded of it for several years to come. That's just how deep things may cut with a woman.

So as this pertains to listening, a wife appreciates a husband who genuinely has her best interests at heart and he takes the time out to become aware of what's on her heart and mind by listening to her.

One of the best examples of this was what shared when Marilyn and Billy were guests on *Maverick Media (on Blog Talk Radio)*. Their appearance also coincided with Marilyn's birthday—and just weeks after them celebrating their 40th wedding anniversary.

"One thing [Billy] did beautiful this morning...I was telling him that I had some thoughts on my mind and some concerns that I was trying to deal with, and he sat down and wanted to hear all about them. And that's after forty years," she said. "He wanted me to tell him what was on my heart."

Typically, men are inclined to think about what's only important to them. Women are just as guilty. That is the selfish nature within all of us. However, Billy responded, "[Marilyn] is my thing. She is what I have to deal with. Her point comes first."

Although I shared with Billy and Marilyn that I did something earlier that week out of volition that my wife appreciated, I recall my behavior from an incident that occurred in 1999 that was the converse to listening to my wife with sincerity. In that scenario, my wife and I were hosts of a gathering and we had some people who stopped by our house prior to them going to the venue. I was in the living room working on printed material. My wife was headed for the kitchen when she mentioned something to me (that to this day I still have no idea what she said), but I never responded.

The guest was stunned. "Didn't you hear her?"

I didn't respond to the guest, either. Or, if I did, I talked around it and continued what I was doing. Needless to say, my wife reminded me of that exchange for many years to come. I understand now that it did not cast a favorable shadow upon my marriage or me.

Out of curiosity, I posed the question among my social network contacts whether they felt their spouse or significant other listened to them. More than ninety percent of my respondents were female. Of that, the majority of them felt the man in their life did not listen to them nor took what they had to say seriously.

"Good question," said one female. "I don't think he does because I wouldn't have to repeat myself."

Another woman lamented, "My current relationship is actually on the skids because of this very problem. After being with someone for a longtime it's time to take the relationship to the next fade or bounce, but he's not hearing me when I say it and I am sooooo serious [about] entertaining new prospects as well."

There were few women who responded that their husband (or significant other) listened to them. "The majority of time," one said.

Many husbands are guilty of just outright refusing to take into consideration anything their wives attempt to communicate with them. But it takes a conscious decision that he's going to make the effort to treat his wife with a level of honor—and love—that he expects in return from her. The moment my wife began to sense that I really wanted to make things right with her and our marriage was the day our marriage and the entire family dynamic changed for the good.

The impact was so profound for my wife that she confided in me that she felt as if she was a newlywed once again. There has since been no good thing that she's withheld from me. I noticed that I even had a better perspective toward life because I knew things at home were much better. In short, the hopelessness that I once felt was being replaced with optimism.

Admittedly, I made several superficial attempts in the past in this area. The marital dynamic between my wife and I would appear as favorable for all of about one day and maybe two sexual encounters at the most. During that time, it did not take much before I'd lose my resolve at working on our marriage. In short, I looked for ways to disqualify myself because I had a different idea as to what would really make *me* happy, and myself alone.

My wife's constant complaint was that she was the one who would suggest doing things like reading books, watching television programs, or viewing an Internet site that offered content on enhancing marriages. "When will you do something to say that you're making an effort?" she'd ask.

Sadly, I had no response. I was guilty of ignoring her most of the time, or I was guilty of procrastinating or being easily distracted by finding another project to work on. Trying to reach me she'd say, "You can't expect for me to be responsive to you when you're doing nothing that pours into your marriage or your wife!"

Now why did she have to tell me something like that? I'd fume, "Listen, it doesn't take all that. If that's the case, nobody would have a marriage having to live up to *those* kinds of expectations."

Nonetheless, she posed the question to me, "How long will it take for you to understand that you can't continue the way you're going? I pray that you're not seventy-five before you get it. That would be such a shame for a man with so much potential..."

Inwardly I agreed with her but only so much. There were many occasions in which I thought there had to be a better way without having to subject myself to something so stupid. The truth is that there are never any shortcuts in life. I would not expect someone to do that with me, but I was steadfast and determined to figure out some detour or alternate route to my marriage. And that was when I was willing to do things in a pseudo-ethically and morally upright manner.

Few of my efforts were actually pleasing to my wife. There were times she went along with them, but eventually she would tell me that I wasn't getting the job done as a husband. Ultimately, I was frustrated at myself because I saw other aspects of my life failing to materialize as I had envisioned. That's a difficult way of living in a household when there's a cloud of dysfunction, discord, and disunity hovering over it.

So one of the benefits to listening to your spouse with sincerity is that you begin to develop and cultivate trust among each other. There is also an increased degree of respect and admiration. If your marriage is in that state of dysfunction, discord and disunity, this is one of the little things that might re-ignite the spark that once led both of you down that aisle of matrimony.

Okay, so you say you're not married. I haven't left you out. Let's presume that you've been in a lengthy relationship. This chapter might help you filter out whether the person you're with is really the one for your life.

I've heard that love is blind and lust not only blinds, but lust makes a drunken fool out of us because we lose all common sense. So perhaps this is something that is good to consider in moments of sobriety.

Let us all be sober!

IN REVIEW:

- One of the benefits to listening to your spouse with sincerity is that you begin to develop and cultivate trust among each other.

- It takes a conscious decision that husbands will make the effort to treat their wives with a level of honor—and love—that they expect in return.

- For any relationship that's worth having, one must put talk and thoughts into action.

Husbands, Listen to Your Wives (in the Bedroom)

When a man fails to listen to his wife, and he makes no effort at understanding her, the couple's sex life is certain to be most disappointing. Sexual frustration—or the lack of satisfaction—is easily among the three biggest issues within a marriage. The other two are money and simply getting along.

I once mocked and scoffed with regularity examples of women who said their husbands were loving and totally supportive not knowing that a couple of the attributes that these men probably possessed—or developed if it had not been a part of them—was the ability to listen to and understand their wives. I'm not going to say that I was envious of those men. I will say that I was ignorant of making application of it, and it didn't make for a blissful situation in my marriage.

There are good husbands who have done all the things that they've known to be right in their marriage, yet there is always room for improvement. Ask a woman what she wants most in a man, most will say money, gifts, and great sex are nice. But what she wants most after a man loving her for whom she is as a woman is a man who listens to her and understands her; it is the foundation for intimacy that leads to mutual fulfillment in the marriage bedroom.

Says one female social network respondent, "I love a man who understands and listens to his woman, with the great sex... Because if you can't listen [to] and understand me why be with me. [That's the key word to everyone (in a) friendship or relationship: to understand and listen.]"

A wife is more than capable of telling her husband what satisfies her in the bedroom during sex. Most times, the husband who succeeds at satisfying his wife will start the work long before they've reached a moment of intercourse.

"You know what I would really love for you to do for me, honey?" the wife queries her husband.

"What's that?"

"For once, I would really love for you to surprise me when I come home from work, you having sent the kids over to your sister's place for the night; you've either prepared dinner, or had something delivered, and lit some candles. Then you've set the mood with some nice music. But most of all, I want to hear you tell me how much you really love me. That would really make my day."

"Now why would I have to do all that?"

"Because, if you really care about me enjoying sex as much as you want having it, you would make the effort and do those things. I'm not asking a lot out of you. I'm not asking you to buy me a diamond ring or a new car. I'm just asking you to do small, thoughtful things."

In the scenario mentioned, the wife has given her husband the keys to getting what he desires as well as for her. There are many husbands who will dismiss what his wife just suggested as her nagging or trying to get him to do something that seems utterly stupid. Their pride will tell them all that is not necessary; she's just leading him along to do all that she asked of him so that she can have the upper hand during sex.

There are some husbands who just might take up on the wife's suggestion just to see if she might respond. There is a good chance that it will be more than worth his while.

Years ago, I discovered the word relationship means to relate, intertwine, have association with, and to link. This discovery occurred while I was still a single man, known for wandering in and out of various encounters with women, and leaving a trail of broken hearts and damaged emotions behind me. The various connotations of relationship sounded nice. It was even nice to realize that we all needed people in our lives, and a way of expressing that was in the way we interact with others.

Then there was my discovery of examples in the Bible where husbands benefitted from listening to their wives. That made for another nice nugget of information. I was a man increasing in knowledge but without making any application of it – many husbands fit a similar description.

My wife hinted at me in various ways that a husband's inability or unwillingness to listen can create chasms in his marriage, resulting in unresolved issues with his wife that is not known until it is too late. Attitudes, anger, and acrimony are some of things that are added to an already potentially volatile mix.

When a woman talks about making love, I'll venture to say that many men, including myself in times past, have drawn a blank on more than a couple of occasions. *Like what in the hell is she talking about. And what romance novel she's gotten all wrapped up into?*

It's taken much of my adult life to reach an understanding of what lovemaking is truly about. In my opinion, it involves commitment and relationship, and it is an expression of patience and kindness. It is a sincere expression of affection. It is a yielding of trust to an individual, sharing some of the most personal and intimate things with my partner (in my case, wife). It is also me giving of myself for her joy and pleasure; yet if it is truly love, she'll also reciprocate it.

Lovemaking is well behaved, sensual, and decent; it is not something demented borne out of acts of cruelty and selfishness. Lovemaking will edify, embrace, and excite the person you're with:

- It is also an intense, emotional, and intimate encounter.

- The culmination of foreplay derived by physical, verbal, non-verbal, and emotional contact.

- The opportunity to see your partner as he or she is; the acceptance of that person as he or she is; the faith that each partner is capable of fulfilling each other's desire.

- An occasion to discover a partner's threshold for pleasure and fulfillment.

- An atmosphere that is created and a stimulus to sexual expression.

Ultimately, making love will always accomplish its goal of achieving oneness in spirit, soul, and body. As with many of life's pursuits, a marriage will always be what both partners make of it. There have been many things that I've had to do that changed the direction in my marriage.

A key factor in it was taking the initiative of listening to my wife.

Endnotes

[1]Boyd, Sr., Frederick Douglas, *Non-Verbal Behaviors of Effective Teachers of At-Risk African-American Male Middle School Students* (Virginia Tech, April 2000)

[2]Boyd, Sr., Frederick Douglas, *Non-Verbal Behaviors of Effective Teachers of At-Risk African-American Male Middle School Students* (Virginia Tech, April 2000) p. 12-15.

[3]Boyd, Sr., Frederick Douglas, *Non-Verbal Behaviors of Effective Teachers of At-Risk African-American Male Middle School Students* (Virginia Tech, April 2000) p. 12-15.

[4]Amen, Daniel G., Md., *The Brain in Love* (New York: Three Rivers Press) p. 63

[5]Amen, Daniel G., Md., *The Brain in Love* (New York: Three Rivers Press) p. 78

[6]Chartrand, Tanya; Dalton, Amy; Fitzsimmons, Gavin, "Nonconscious relationship reactance: When significant others prime opposing goals" *Journal of Experimental Social Psychology (2006)* p. 719-727.

References

Amen, Daniel G., Md., *The Brain in Love* (New York: Three Rivers Press)

Evans, Jimmy, "Men Receiving Influence from Wives" *Marriage Today*. www.marriagetoday.com

Grigsby, Connie, "Get Your Husband to Listen to You" by Belinda Elliott. Christian Broadcasting Network (CBN) www.cbn.com

Hall, Judith and Knapp, Mark, *Nonverbal Communication in Human Interaction* (1992, 3rd Edition)

Indiana University, "Men Do Hear -- But Differently Than Women" *ScienceDaily* (November 29, 2000).

Kessler, Ronald, "Facing your fear" *USA Today Weekend* by Mary Ellin Lerner (October 1, 2000).

McCoo, Marilyn and Billy Davis, Jr., *Up, Up, and Away: How We Found Love, Faith, and Lasting Marriage in the Entertainment World* (Chicago: Northfield Publishing, 2004)

McShane, Larry, "Candidate Obama didn't think so on his 'Yes, we can!' campaign slogan" *New York Daily News* (Sept. 19, 2009).

New King James Version Bible, Thomas Nelson Publishers (1990).

Stritof, Sheri and Bob, *Reasons Why Your Spouse Won't Listen to You.* About.com Guide to Marriage.

Stritof, Sheri and Bob, *When Your Spouse Won't Listen.* About. com Guide to Marriage.

Stritof, Sheri and Bob, *Tips for When You Have to Talk.* About. com Guide to Marriage.

Stritof, Sheri and Bob, *Talk with Each Other - Not at Each Other.* About.com Guide to Marriage.

Tannen, Deborah, "Sex, Lies and Conversation; Why Is It So Hard for Men and Women to Talk to Each Other?" *Washington Post* (June. 24, 1990).

Webster's Encyclopedic Dictionary (1993).

Xpress Yourself Publishing
A Publisher of Fine Books
and
2008 AALAS Independent Publishing House of the Year

Visit us online:
www.xpressyourselfpublishing.com

Follow Us on Twitter:
www.Twitter.com/Xpress_Yourself

Join Us On Facebook:
www.Facebook.com/XpressYourselfPublishing

Join Us On MySpace:
www.MySpace.com/XpressYourselfPublishing

Blog with Us:
www.XpressYourselfPublishing.blogspot.com

Receive Our Newsletter:
www.XpressYourselfPublishing.org

LaVergne, TN USA
27 July 2010
191056LV00002B/38/P